WALKING IN ABRUZZO

About the Author

Stuart Haines is a walker, mountain lover, guidebook writer, project manager and occasional viticulturalist. His explorations of the remoter corners of central Italy began in 2004, following many years of climbing and adventuring in the Alps, North America and his native UK. Since 2007 he has been based between Bristol, England, and Casa La Rocca, the country house in the heart of Abruzzo that he renovated with his partner, Hil. The house offers self-catered accommodation for visitors to the region and is the base for Stuart's support service for walkers, cyclists and everyone who comes to discover the grandeur of Abruzzo for themselves – route advice, drop-offs and pick-ups, pack transport, overnight booking and the organic Montepulciano d'Abruzzo house wine all available under one roof – www.casalarocca.it.

WALKING IN ABRUZZO

GRAN SASSO, MAIELLA AND ABRUZZO NATIONAL PARKS, AND SIRENTE-VELINO REGIONAL PARK

by Stuart Haines

JUNIPER HOUSE, MURLEY MOSS,
OXENHOLME ROAD, KENDAL, CUMBRIA LA9 7RL
www.cicerone.co.uk

© Stuart Haines 2019
Second edition 2019
ISBN: 978 1 85284 978 8
First edition 2011

Printed in China on behalf of Latitude Press Ltd
A catalogue record for this book is available from the British Library.
All photographs are by the author unless otherwise stated.

Route mapping by Lovell Johns www.lovelljohns.com
Contains OpenStreetMap.org data © OpenStreetMap
contributors, CC-BY-SA. NASA relief data courtesy of ESRI

Dedication

For Hil

Updates to this guide

While every effort is made by our authors to ensure the accuracy of guidebooks
as they go to print, changes can occur during the lifetime of an edition. Any
updates that we know of for this guide will be on the Cicerone website (www.
cicerone.co.uk/978/updates), so please check before planning your trip. We
also advise that you check information about such things as transport, accommodation and shops locally. Even rights of way can be altered over time.

The route maps in this guide are derived from publicly available data, data-
bases and crowd-sourced data. As such they have not been through the detailed
checking procedures that would generally be applied to a published map from
an official mapping agency, although naturally we have reviewed them closely
in the light of local knowledge as part of the preparation of this guide.

We are always grateful for information about any discrepancies between
a guidebook and the facts on the ground, sent by email to updates@cicerone.
co.uk or by post to Cicerone, Juniper House, Murley Moss, Oxenholme Road,
Kendal, LA9 7RL.

Register your book: To sign up to receive free updates, special offers and
GPX files where available, register your book at www.cicerone.co.uk.

Front cover: Monte Ocre ridge looking towards Monte Cagno and Monte Sirente
(Walk 37)

CONTENTS

Mountain safety

Every mountain walk has its dangers, and those described in this guidebook are no exception. All who walk or climb in the mountains should recognise this and take responsibility for themselves and their companions along the way. The author and publisher have made every effort to ensure that the information contained in this guide was correct when it went to press, but, except for any liability that cannot be excluded by law, they cannot accept responsibility for any loss, injury or inconvenience sustained by any person using this book.

International distress signal *(emergency only)*
Six blasts on a whistle (and flashes with a torch after dark) spaced evenly for one minute, followed by a minute's pause. Repeat until an answer is received. The response is three signals per minute followed by a minute's pause.

Helicopter rescue
The following signals are used to communicate with a helicopter:

 Help needed:
raise both arms
above head to
form a 'Y'

 Help not needed:
raise one arm
above head, extend
other arm downward

Emergency telephone numbers
If telephoning from the UK the dialling code is 0039

Carabinieri: tel 0165 84 22 25
Emergency Services: tel 118

Weather reports
tel 0165 44 113
www.ilmeteo.it

Mountain rescue can be very expensive – be adequately insured.

Monte Prena from the Vado di Ferruccio

Symbols used on route maps

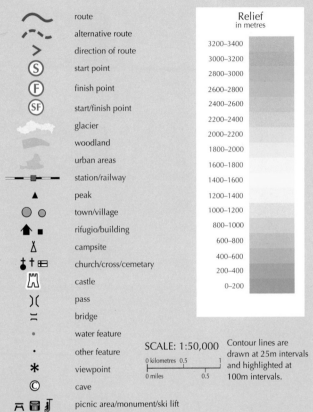

~	route
- - -	alternative route
>	direction of route
(S)	start point
(F)	finish point
(SF)	start/finish point
	glacier
	woodland
	urban areas
—■—	station/railway
▲	peak
⬤ ⬤	town/village
↑ ■	rifugio/building
⚊	campsite
↑ † ▥	church/cross/cemetary
🏰	castle
)(	pass
≍	bridge
•	water feature
·	other feature
*	viewpoint
©	cave
🛋 🏛 ⌇	picnic area/monument/ski lift

Relief
in metres

3200–3400	
3000–3200	
2800–3000	
2600–2800	
2400–2600	
2200–2400	
2000–2200	
1800–2000	
1600–1800	
1400–1600	
1200–1400	
1000–1200	
800–1000	
600–800	
400–600	
200–400	
0–200	

SCALE: 1:50,000

0 kilometres 0.5

0 miles 0.5

Contour lines are drawn at 25m intervals and highlighted at 100m intervals.

GPX files

GPX files for all routes can be downloaded for free at www.cicerone.co.uk/978/GPX.

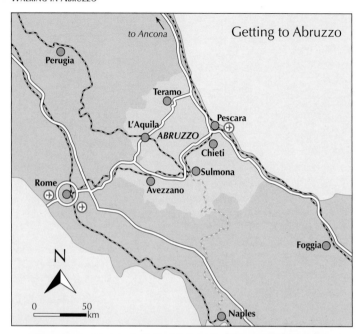

Corno Grande group from Monte di Mezzo (Walk 20)

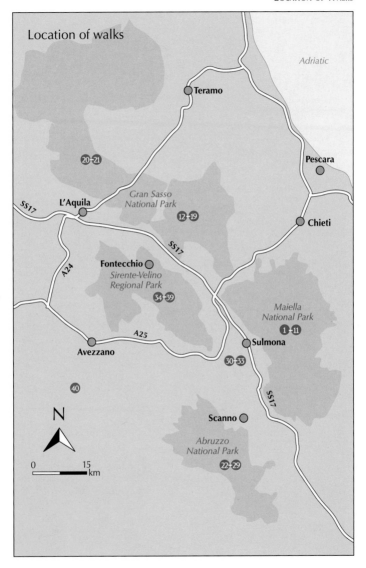

Location of walks

Adriatic

Teramo

Pescara

20-21

Gran Sasso
National Park

SS17

L'Aquila

12-19

Chieti

SS17

Fontecchio

A24

Sirente-Velino
Regional Park

34-39

Maiella
National Park

1-11

A25

Sulmona

Avezzano

30-33

40

SS17

N

Scanno

0   15
km

Abruzzo
National Park

22-29

Entering the open valley behind Monte Ocre (Walk 37)

INTRODUCTION

Campo Imperatore from Sella di Monte Aquila (Walks 14 and 16)

It's 7.30pm. You are standing on the tower of the isolated medieval castle, Rocca Calascio, set dramatically at 1500m on a narrow ridge in the heart of Abruzzo. Fading light is softening the seemingly endless ridges, peaks and valleys that lie in every direction; the silence is underlined by occasional barking from a hamlet below.

One other building stands nearby. The beautiful octagonal church of Madonna della Pietà is isolated against the dramatic south east face of Corno Grande, the apex of the Apennines, 16km to the north and 1500m higher still.

It's early June. The day has been hot and sunny, although the hours on the trail were eased by a gentle breeze rising from the Adriatic. The air is still warm but it's time for a light sweater.

This is the centre of the Gran Sasso National Park. The peak and west flank of Corno Grande blaze in the sinking sun while the steep, stark east wall has fallen into shadow. You think about yesterday, when you stood on that summit and fed sweetcorn kernels to the choughs. You felt that you could see from one side of Italy to the other, while all the mountains of Abruzzo were ranged around.

Now, slanting rays light up the ancient village of Carapelle Calvisio, lying on a lower ridge to the south. The forest has darkened, providing a fine background to the glowing tones of the beautiful old buildings.

The peace is extraordinary and the view immense. It is easy to understand why 10th-century barons chose

13

Corno Piccolo from the west ridge of Corno Grande (Walk 14)

this place to raise their fortress – the highest and surely the most picturesque in Italy.

The soft clatter of an old tractor draws your gaze to the valley floor. It is moving slowly down a white lane through strips of lentil and potato fields, along the route of the famous Sentiero Italia – a footpath that runs from the Dolomites to the tip of Sicily. Not that you can imagine undertaking such a walk when there is so much to be explored in just the landscape you can see!

Imperceptibly, the far ridges turn to abstract layers of green, blue and purple, capped by the reddening sky. The peaks of the Maiella and the Abruzzo national parks, way south, grow a little larger as they become silhouettes on the horizon. Wispy cloud has gathered on the shoulders of Monte Amaro, the crown of the Maiella massif and, at 2800m, the

region's second highest point. You look away and then back – it has gone as quickly as it formed.

The Peligna basin, separating the three national parks, lies below the steep west slopes of the Maiella. It's too dark now to make out Sulmona, the main town of central Abruzzo, but tomorrow you will walk towards it. In two days' time you will arrive there, tired and a little regretful, to spend your last night before catching the train back to Rome.

A church bell tolls in Castel del Monte, a few kilometres to the north east. It's one of the highest villages in the Apennines and gateway to the magnificent mountain plain of Campo Imperatore, which you spent most of the day crossing. It has been a memorable day, with the countryside carpeted in wildflowers and populated by semi-wild horses, flocks of sheep and creamy coated, ever-watchful

Abruzzo sheep dogs. The four shepherds you greeted were the only people you met – more like a little corner of Tibet than Italy. It seemed a barren, wild place from the heights of Corno Grande, but as you wandered across the undulating pasture the early summer flora, recently emerged from beneath spring snow, was a rich surprise.

Thoughts of food and cold beer intrude on your reverie. Settling your pack for the last time, you watch the tower catch the last of the sun. In the west the long, darkening ridge of Monte Sirente, in the Sirente-Velino Regional Park, forms the final wall enclosing this secluded world of peaks and plains, hilltop villages, forests and ancient towns.

You stroll down to the cluster of stone houses and cobbled passages below. The once-abandoned hamlet is being brought quietly back to life by a few dedicated families who, with national park and regional support, are slowly renovating the tumbledown buildings. One of the first to re-open was Rifugio Rocca Calascio, where your meal, bath and bed await. Earlier you passed through the medieval village of Santo Stefano di Sessanio, now almost fully restored to its Medici heyday. Abruzzo's conservation and renewal policies are bearing remarkable fruit.

Children's laughter and the smell of pasta sauce are the only directions you need. A fox sneaking across the hillside sets the dogs off again. This is a special place – an astounding protected landscape, criss-crossed with tracks and trails, waiting for adventurous spirits to discover it for themselves.

ABRUZZO

Despite its central location and close proximity to Rome, Abruzzo is one of Italy's least known and populated regions – a spectacular and harmonious blend of snowy mountains, grassy plains and forested canyons; of hillside olive groves, vineyards and long sandy beaches. Its natural riches are protected in three national parks, one regional park and many smaller reserves. Thousands of years of history are reflected in a multitude of abandoned castles, hilltop villages and ancient farmsteads; religious dedication echoed in splendid abbeys, silent churches and remote hermitages.

It's a wonderful place to get to know. The Abruzzesi are resourceful, respectful and welcoming people – with a sure view of their global future but a firm sense of their history and tradition. Neither northern nor southern, the spirit of Abruzzo is its own.

The wild and high Apennine ridges form the grain of the land. Two thirds of the area is mountainous and one third is protected. The claim to be the greenest region in Europe is well founded.

Ancient sheep droves run hundreds of kilometres from the coastal plain of Puglia northwards into the mountain pastures of Abruzzo – the traditional routes of the great bi-annual migration of flocks and shepherds known as the *transumanza*.

The mountains are home to marvellous and rare plants and animals. The highest peaks of peninsular Italy are here, their slopes supporting ski resorts and an extensive network of summer trekking and mountain biking trails. The mountains fall to the Adriatic, the intervening hills covered in vines, olives and orchards; the coastline itself is developed with resorts offering warm, safe bathing – beach bars, sun shades and loungers as far as you can see.

The region is divided into four provinces, each named after its capital town – L'Aquila, Chieti, Pescara and Teramo. **L'Aquila** is also the seat of regional government and Abruzzo's cultural centre. Its university can trace its roots back over 500 years. It's a refined and beautiful city situated high on the flanks of the Gran Sasso mountains and continuing ever more quickly to recover from the major earthquake of 2009. The largest settlement, though, is relatively modern **Pescara**, where over 120,000 live in new apartment blocks and villas on the long Adriatic shore.

Twenty-three of Abruzzo's villages have been designated among the most beautiful in Italy – the highest number of all the regions of the country. Despite this, Abruzzo remains a largely unfashionable

corner of Italy and the better for it. Spared overwhelming touristic icons (no leaning tower or grand baroque fountain), it has revealed itself slowly to the outside world. Development is at a steady pace. There are manufacturing industries, motorway connections, a large coastal city (Pescara, a favoured holiday spot of Italians), sophisticated restaurants and modern shopping malls but, mostly, low key. What can't escape your attention, though, is the empty mountainous countryside – a magnificent unspoilt landscape to savour and explore.

GEOLOGICAL HISTORY

The Apennine mountains of Abruzzo are formed predominately of limestone and other calcareous sediments dating from the Mesozoic period in geological history – between 250 million years and 67 million years ago. The sediments were laid down in the warm, calm waters of the long-gone Tethys Sea and marine fossils are commonly found in the region. This was the age of the dinosaurs and their relics, too, have been uncovered.

Mountain building began very recently in geological terms and is a process that continues today. The tectonic make-up of peninsular Italy is complex but, essentially, the Adriatic plate is being dragged south westwards (subducted) beneath the adjacent plate, causing the sedimentary rocks above the line of subduction to be crumpled upwards, forming the

The upper part of the Celano gorge (Walk 35)

Apennine chain. Long considered to be a result of the same event that created the Alps, it is now known that the Apennines are quite independent geologically and were formed much later. The area remains seismically active as the stresses built up during continuing plate movement are released with sometimes shattering consequences.

The grain of the land runs north west to south east – perpendicular to the direction of movement of the Adriatic plate. The upthrust limestone massifs have been sculpted by ice and water and eroded into sharp peaks and rounded plateaus, gashed by narrow ravines and separated by high grassy basins where once large lakes lay.

HUMAN HISTORY

Human occupation can be traced back to Neolithic times. In the millennia BC, present-day Abruzzo was the home of many Italic tribes – notably the Frentani, the Vestini, the Marsi and the Paeligni. The tribes united to resist Etruscan and Roman attempts to annex their lands, forming a joint base at present-day Corfinio, near Sulmona, which they named Italia. After a final defeat during the Social Wars, the tribes aligned with the Romans to play an important role in the development and sustainment of their empire. (Ovid, the famous Roman poet, was born in Sulmona in 43BC.) The name Italia, however, lived on and was eventually adopted by the reunified nation in the 19th century.

17

The Tre Portoni from Monte Focalone (Walk 8)

Following the fall of the Roman Empire and the spread of Christianity, the history of Abruzzo becomes complex and confused. Initially the area fell under the control of the Lombards, as a part of their Duchy of Spoleto, which was then given by Charlemagne to the church. This era saw the establishment of many religious houses – great abbeys and cathedrals as well as monastic retreats.

Then came the Normans, whose control reached to southern Italy. They established the Kingdom of Sicily, of which Abruzzo became a part. The Normans ceded the kingdom to the Swabians, who in 1268 were in turn defeated by the House of Anjou. During Angevin rule, Abruzzo became a part of the Kingdom of Naples. The University of L'Aquila was founded in 1458.

In the early 16th century, the Spanish arrived to take control. They merged the Kingdom of Naples into the larger Kingdom of the Two Sicilies. After 1700 Spain itself and its territories came to be ruled by the House of Bourbon. Bourbon rule of the Kingdom of the Two Sicilies continued uninterrupted until the Risorgimento in 1860 – the unification of Italy, spearheaded by Garibaldi's army, and the foundation of the modern state.

In the modern era, Abruzzo knew desperate poverty following the Second World War. During this time many thousands of families emigrated to North and South America, Australia and other parts of Europe, to be followed by relatively recent economic recovery and development. Abruzzo became a separate region of Italy in the 1960s and is now the most prosperous of all in the official south.

ANIMALS AND BIRDS

The remoteness and height of the Abruzzo mountains, the depths of its native forest and the careful protection afforded by national and regional parks have created one of Italy's most wonderful wildlife refuges.

Clinging on in the quietest corners of the Abruzzo National Park (and, perhaps, the Maiella and Sirente-Velino) is the Marsican brown bear. It is feared there may be just 50–60 individuals left, and you are unlikely to see one. Evidence of their passing might be encountered though – paw prints and scat. You are even more unlikely to meet a European lynx, but it has been spotted and is thought to have a reasonable chance of survival provided levels of protection are maintained. Wild cats and pine martens also live a rare and secluded life in the forests.

In the same areas, grey wolves are doing better. Although still rare, their numbers are slowly increasing (between 1500 and 2000 individuals in the Apennines, most of which are in Abruzzo), and tracks at least can be spotted in the more remote areas.

Easier to come across in all three national parks are Abruzzi chamois living in large family groups on the bare rocks above the tree line. Walks 1, 7, 8, 16 and 23 are recommended for a good chance of seeing them.

Red deer and roe deer are relatively common throughout the forested areas. The magnificent sound and sight of rutting red deer stags in the autumn is unforgettable. Walk 23 offers a good prospect of the experience at this time of year.

If you are lucky, otters can be seen in the rivers of the Maiella National Park. The Orfento valley is a potential spot – see Walk 5.

The most common of the large mammals is the wild boar – since its reintroduction it has become well

Family of chamois on Passo Cavuto (Walk 23)

established. You may come across them in the forest (if they haven't sensed your arrival first – they are shy).

In the skies above the wilder parts of the region, golden eagles drift on the thermals. The Celano gorge (Walk 35), Colli Alti (Walk 29) and the Fara San Martino gorge (Walk 1) are good spots for viewing. Peregrine falcons swoop and plunge above the cliffs where they nest – try the old quarries on Walk 33 which are a favourite haunt. In the woods, the cries of woodpeckers and jays are common, while on the high crags the sharp whistle of choughs is an equally frequent part of the mountain soundtrack.

Fox in the Val Chiarino (Walk 19)

PLANTS AND FLOWERS

The mountains and remoter parts of Abruzzo are a plant lovers' paradise. The protected and relatively undeveloped landscape, the variety of habitats and the climatic conditions sustain a rich flora – from resin-scented Mediterranean scrub, through to magnificent beech and oak forest, and up to delicate, brilliantly coloured alpine meadows.

In the mountains, the retreating snows trigger an explosion of bright spring-time growth – crocus, mountain pansies, gentians, poppies, beautiful creeping alpines and, in places, the Apennine edelweiss. Lower down, the woods and valleys fill with a profusion of flowering plants and shrubs from the end of winter to late summer, with a variety of orchids prominent. The extensive beech, pine, oak and birch forests are a spectacle in their own right, and in the autumn present vivid fireburst shades of orange, red and yellow.

The compact Abruzzo National Park provides a home for over 2000 species, including the black pine and the characteristic but rare lady's slipper orchid. Mountain, or mugo, pine grows thickly in places in the Maiella National Park. In the Sirente-Velino Regional Park, the purple Marsican iris stands tall in May and June, while the high plain of Campo Imperatore in the Gran Sasso National Park is tinted lilac by a vast carpet of crocuses every spring.

Wild flowers and ferns in the Maiella

FOOD AND DRINK

The pleasure of walking in Abruzzo is perfectly complemented by enjoyment of the local cuisine – the freshest plate of antipasti, followed by the speciality house pasta dish and, if you have room, a meat or fish main course. The desserts can rarely be resisted, and the evening is best ended with coffee and a glass of the village amaretto. A visit to the local pizzeria or café will result in an equally satisfying experience – Italians take eating and drinking seriously!

A simple mix of mountain robustness, fertile hill country and the riches of the sea has produced a fine and varied regional gastronomy – the pasta, lamb, pecorino cheese and fish dishes are renowned throughout Italy, as is the characteristic Montepulciano d'Abruzzo red wine. There are delights to be found in the village *alimentari*, in the next-door bar, on every restaurant menu and, especially, on market-day stalls.

Abruzzo is a famous pasta region, home to De Cecco and Delverde, two of Italy's leading producers. *Chitarra* is a typically Abruzzese form – square-shaped strands made by pushing a pasta sheet through wires strung across a wooden box. Pasta and bean stew (*pasta fagioli*) delicately flavoured with fresh herbs is a simple delight at the end of a long day's walk.

From the flocks of mountain sheep come pecorino and riccota, among the finest in Italy. Both cheeses find their way into many regional recipes. Local production still plays an important role, and cheesemakers may be encountered on walks across the high plains. The traditional significance of sheep rearing is seen, too, in the local passion for *arrosticcini* – skewers of small lamb kebabs grilled over an open charcoal-filled trough. Roast pork (*porchetta*) is also a regional favourite.

Pescara is the home of a large fishing fleet and the quayside market

21

is a fine sight when the boats come in. Fish stews, risottos, soups and simple grilled fillets taste delicious when so fresh. Again, local recipes feature strongly in the region's restaurants.

Other regional specialities are fine olives; saffron from the Navelli plain; red garlic and sugared almonds (*confetti*) from Sulmona; lentils from Santo Stefano; polenta made from maize; truffles, chestnuts and porcini mushrooms from the forests; and *cima di rapa* – a green leafed vegetable prepared quite deliciously.

Wine production, too, is a regional obsession. Montepulciano d'Abruzzo is the local red wine and Trebbiano and Pecorino are the whites. Much of the production is on a small scale for family use but the commercial wineries produce many memorable bottles.

Nearly every village in the region has its *festa*, usually in the summer – a celebration of the local speciality food with music, wine and, at the end of the night, lots of fireworks.

WALKING IN ABRUZZO

Abruzzo is wonderful walking country. It is one of the wildest and least populated regions of Italy, with 169 peaks over 2000m, long mountain ridges, high plains and deep gorges, huge forests of native beech, oak and pine and gentle fertile valleys. The highest points in peninsular Italy and the southernmost glacier in Europe are all here.

This beautiful natural environment is maintained to a remarkable extent in the region's three national parks, one regional park and many smaller reserves. Almost a third of the entire region is afforded protected status of one form or other. The parks cover the four main mountain massifs; they correspond also to the main walking areas, although there are many fine routes throughout the region.

The **Gran Sasso e Monte della Laga National Park** covers an area of over 150,000 hectares in the north of the region, one of the largest national parks in Italy. Its spectacular high point is Corno Grande, at 2912m the highest point in the Apennines. In a wild corrie sheltered by the three peaks of Corno Grande lies the small and fast-disappearing Calderone glacier, the most southerly in Europe. From the foot of the mountain, the magnificent high plain of Campo Imperatore stetches away for 25km. With an average altitude of 1400m, the plain covers an empty 80km^2.

The **Maiella National Park** lies in the south east and covers the area of the high and wild Amaro massif, the nearby Morrone massif and the ridges and plains that run up to them. Monte Amaro, at 2793m, is a barren and exhilarating place – the second highest point in the Apennines. The park is just 30km from the Adriatic, and the south east slopes are incised by a series of spectacular gorges. Ancient monasteries and hermits' retreats are

Monte Amaro from a meadow on Walk 9

hidden away, blended into the remote cliff faces.

The long-established **Abruzzo, Lazio e Molise National Park** lies in the south west of the region. It's a relatively small area but its high peaks and ridges and remote forested valleys harbour an internationally famous wildlife. Its biodiversity is as remarkable as its beauty. In the ancient forests and on the bare crags of the Upper Sangro and its side valleys live bears, wolves, chamois, boar, lynx and eagles.

The **Sirente-Velino** massif in the west of Abruzzo is (merely) a regional park, but you would be pushed to tell the difference. The management of its contrasting natural habitats – gentle meadows, deep gorges, high mountain walls and spectacular sub-alpine summits – has been equally effective in creating a rewarding walking area.

All the parks are covered by a network of established paths. In addition, lovely routes lie along the thousands of country lanes, tracks and droves and across open hillside and meadow, especially in the areas beyond the park boundaries.

Waymarks are usually paint splashes (red, or red and white) but can be cairns, signposts or even plastic strands tied to branches. A route indicated as 'waymarked' usually has good or adequate signing (when combined with the recommended map and route description), although occasionally it is poor. Marking can be inconsistent or old, especially where more than one authority is involved – perhaps the national park and the Club Alpino Italiano (CAI) and the Corpo Forestale dello Stato (CFS) vying with different colour schemes! Be careful – but don't be put off.

Rifugios (mountain huts) are spread across the upland area but most are locked or spartan bivouacs. Many are shepherds' huts or, if operated by the CAI or park authority, have no guardian (warden) and the key (often available only to members) must be collected beforehand. There are some notable exceptions – see 'Places to base yourself', below.

WHEN TO GO

Abruzzo is a coastal and upland region where seasons are remarkably varied. Overall the climate is typically Mediterranean, but altitude brings a big variation. Winter in the mountains is reliably cold. There are 10 ski resorts (little known outside Italy) and the main walking areas are deeply covered in snow well into the spring – fantastic for cross-country skiing and snowshoeing! Summer is reliably hot and dry; the seasonal rivers disappear and the hillsides turn tinder-brown. Spectacular lightening storms and localised downpours bring relief when the atmosphere becomes too charged. Between the two, spring and autumn are usually mild and can be damp.

The walking season begins in late spring and goes into autumn – late April to late October. Ideal, perhaps, are the months of May, June and September, either side of high summer (which can be very hot). July and August can be very enjoyable too, and are (relatively speaking) the busiest times on the trail. April and October should not be dismissed as they offer solitude, often perfect conditions and the riches of the changing seasons.

Even March and November can see spells of clear, settled weather.

GETTING THERE

Abruzzo is easy to reach, both from other regions of Italy and from abroad, and its main centres are well connected by road and rail.

The **airport at Pescara** is served by several low-cost airlines that fly from countries in Europe and offer internal flights to destinations in Italy. For most of the year, Ryanair (www.ryanair.com) flies five days a week from London Stansted and Frankfurt, four days a week from Brussels and twice a week from Dusseldorf, Malta and Barcelona. Wizz Air (https://wizzair.com) flies twice a week from Bucharest, and Mistral Air (www.mistralair.it) flies four times a week from Tirana in Albania. Internally, Ryanair and Alitalia (www.alitalia.com) both fly twice a day from Milan, while Mistral Air flies twice a week from Palermo, Catania and Cagliari. Blue Air (www.blueairweb.com) flies three times a week from Turin.

Pescara airport is connected to the city railway station by a frequent bus service. For more information, visit the airport website: www.abruzzoairport.com.

Ancona airport is about 1hr north of Abruzzo by motorway and is connected by fast trains to Pescara. Lufthansa (www.lufthansa.com) connects Ancona daily with Munich, while Ryanair offers four flights a week from London Stansted and two a week from Brussels. Ancona is connected to Rome with two or three flights a day. For details visit www. aeroportomarche.it.

Naples airport (www.aeroporto dinapoli.it) is well served from many UK, European and worldwide destinations. The city is connected to Abruzzo (Sulmona, Chieti and Pescara) by express coach (www.satambus.it) that operates four or five times a day and takes about 3hr.

Accessing Abruzzo via **Rome's two airports**, **Ciampino** and the bigger **Fiumicino**, is also simple and offers links to all corners of the world as well as Italy. easyJet (www.easyjet. com) uses Fiumicino for flights from Bristol, Luton and London Gatwick in the UK. Ryanair operates mainly from Ciampino and serves Edinburgh, Glasgow, East Midlands, Manchester and London Stansted in the UK. Liverpool is connected to Fiumicino

by Blue Air, Manchester by Jet2.com (www.jet2.com), and Cardiff is connected by Flybe (www.flybe.com).

Both British Airways (www.british airways.com) and Alitalia fly to Fiumicino from London Heathrow several times a day and can be competitive with the low-cost operators. British Airways also serves Fiumicino from London Gatwick.

Cork and Dublin are served directly from Rome. Major cities in Europe, North America, Australia, New Zealand and South Africa are all connected to Rome.

The best start point for flights to Rome is a visit to www.adr.it.

Rome is connected to Abruzzo by **road and rail**. The drive on the A24 motorway from the Rome orbital motorway to the Abruzzo border takes about 40min. To continue to L'Aquila takes a further 40min; to Sulmona a further 1hr or to Pescara a further 1hr 30min. Coaches between Abruzzo

View down Valle Pagano from Monte La Meta (Walk 24)

and Rome are operated by TUA – the region's bus company. Services depart from Tiburtina station in Rome. There is an hourly service to L'Aquila. Pescara and Sulmona are both served directly about six times a day. The full timetable and details can be seen at www.tuabruzzo.it.

Prontobus (www.prontobusitalia. it) operates a very useful direct coach service from Rome's airports to several towns in Abruzzo including Avezzano, Sulmona, Chieti and Pescara.

The train from Rome is a lot slower but offers a very picturesque journey and is surprisingly cheap. It takes about 3hr to reach Sulmona and 4hr for Pescara. The train to L'Aquila involves changing at Terni, taking 3–5hr depending on whether the service to Terni is fast. Most leave from Tiburtina station but some depart from Roma Termini. L'Aquila, Pescara and Sulmona are each served about

five times a day. The timetable and online booking are available at www. trenitalia.com.

GETTING AROUND

There is a good public transport network within Abruzzo, again provided by TUA and by Trenitalia. The websites above provide details of all services. While the bus network is extensive, the train is limited to the line between Rome and Pescara (via Avezzano, Sulmona and Chieti) and the line between Terni and Sulmona which passes through L'Aquila. The Adriatic coast fast line also passes through Abruzzo, linking Pescara with Ancona, Rimini and Bologna to the north and Foggia, Bari and Brindisi to the south.

Unfortunately, once you have arrived at your destination, getting to the start of walks by public transport is either a challenge (with a few noted

The end of the day at Rifugio Campitelli (Walk 24)

exceptions) or impossible. Buses can be infrequent and not well timed for early starts or late, unpredictable finishes. A car is usually the only practical option. The major hire companies are at Pescara and Rome airports and the railway stations. Car hire is also available in L'Aquila, Avezzano and Sulmona. Rates are reasonable if booked in advance and offers are frequent.

Finally, Abruzzo is wonderful cycling country (mountain and road are equally good). If you take or hire a bike, depending on your base, it can solve the problem of reaching the start point.

PLACES TO BASE YOURSELF

There are excellent hotels, B&Bs and self-catering apartments throughout the region. A good start point is the regional tourist organisation's website, www.abruzzoturismo.it. Useful sources for self-catering accommodation are www.holidaylettings.co.uk/abruzzo and www.tripadvisor.com.

Your choice of base will depend on whether you focus your trip on one or two of the parks or whether you intend to visit them all.

Sulmona (www.comune.sulmona.aq.it) is a fine town to stay in or near as it is centrally located between all four parks and is easy to reach. It is a beautiful old place that will keep you diverted on rest days as well as providing a good choice of restaurants, bars and places to sleep – new

and traditional hotels, B&Bs and self-catering. Smaller towns in the Peligna basin are **Popoli**, **Pratola** and **Raiano**, and a number of beautiful villages lie around the edge of the basin, including **Pacentro**, **Pettorano**, **Introdaqua**, **Bugnara**, **Anversa** and **Roccacasale**.

If you intend to concentrate on the Gran Sasso and perhaps the Sirente-Velino parks, then **L'Aquila** (www.comune.laquila.it) is an obvious choice. Easy to reach, especially from Rome, it is a captivating and historic place. L'Aquila was badly affected by the earthquake of 2009, although services are now almost back to previous levels – and perhaps even better. Access to parts of the city may still be restricted, but the return of visitors is vital to its economic recovery.

There are many smaller towns in the north of Abruzzo that are good alternatives. **Celano**, **Ovindoli** and **Rocca di Mezzo** are well placed for the Sirente-Velino, while **Teramo** offers good access to the Gran Sasso and Monti della Laga from the east. A number of villages within the Gran Sasso park have small hotels, B&Bs and self-catering accommodation and at least one restaurant. They include **Santo Stefano**, **Calascio**, **Ofena** and **Castel del Monte** in the south, and **Pietracamela**, **Campotosto** and **Assergi** in the north. **Farindola** offers access from the east. The villages of the Aterno valley between the Gran Sasso and the Sirente-Velino are also well situated – the main ones are **San**

Demetrio, Fontecchio, Santa Maria del Ponte and Acciano.

If walking is to be centred on the Maiella National Park, then four small towns lying between the Amaro and Morrone massifs will each meet your needs. The largest, Caramanico Terme (www.comunecaramanicoterme.it), is an old spa town well served with accommodation and restaurants. To the north lies San Valentino in Abruzzo Citeriore, and to the south is Sant'Eufemia a Maiella. Furthest south is Campo di Giove. A number of small towns lie along the east flank of the Maiella, providing good access to the eastern gorges. They include Palena, Lama dei Peligni, Fara San Martino, Guardiagrele and Pretoro.

Within the Abruzzo National Park is the small town of Pescasseroli (www.comune.pescasseroli.aq.it). Its pretty centre and surrounding area offer many accommodation and eating possibilities. Other villages in

the park with places to stay and eat are Barrea, Villetta Barrea, Civitella Alfedena and Opi. Just outside the park at its south eastern end is the small town of Alfedena. Castel di Sangro in the south of the region would be a good place to stay if you wanted to explore both the Abruzzo and the Maiella parks, as would the ski resort villages of Roccaraso, Rivisondoli and pretty Pescocostanzo.

Special mention needs to be made of the Italian institution that is Agriturismo – rural accommodation, often based on farms or small-holdings, offering meals made with the produce of the establishment or locale. *Agriturismo* is well established in Abruzzo and there are lovely places to stay. A good resource is www.agriturismo.it.

Campers are reasonably well provided for in Abruzzo. Most sites are traditional Italian style, with fixed pitches amongst camper vans,

Rifugio Garibaldi (Walk 16)

caravans and semi-permanent holiday huts, and are popular with large holidaying families. There are a few 'wilder' sites in the national parks. Good lists can be found at www.camping.it.

Finally there are a number of alpine-style **mountain huts** in the most popular higher areas. These can be special places to spend the night, and they allow an extended walk in remoter parts. They provide simple sleeping platforms (take your own bag), a cooked evening meal and breakfast. The CAI website (www.cai.it) has a full list (including unmanaged huts), as does the Abruzzo tourist organisation website and individual park websites. Worth particular mention are Rifugio Franchetti, Rifugio Duca degli Abruzzi and Rifugio Giuseppe Garibaldi in the Corno Grande massif, and Rifugio Sebastiani in the Velino.

DAILY ESSENTIALS

Italy is one of the world's most developed economies, and prices are similar to the rest of the Eurozone, the UK and North America. Some things, however, are typically cheaper – wine, coffee, dinner in a village restaurant, train tickets, shoes (you never know) and going to a football match.

Most shops and offices, including banks and post offices, are open from 8.30am to 1pm and then again from 3.30pm to 7pm. Even village cafés often close for lunch.

Supermarkets, though, are increasingly open throughout the day. ATM machines are easily found in towns and quite often villages. They usually recognise foreign debit cards and will dispense euros. Credit cards are often not accepted by B&Bs and restaurants – keep topped up with cash.

Mobile phone coverage is good in Abruzzo, although you will be out of touch in the remoter valleys. There aren't many public phone boxes – the *telefonino* (mobile phone) has become an essential. The internet, too, is just about everywhere. 4G data network coverage for smartphones is good and there are internet cafés in all of Abruzzo's main towns. Wi-fi connections are usually available in hotels and B&Bs and can often be found in cafés. Some town centres, such as Sulmona, are covered by a municipal wi-fi network.

There isn't a great deal of English spoken in Abruzzo, but someone can usually be found, particularly in a restaurant, hotel or even a mountain hut. You can enjoy a walking holiday with a basic grasp of Italian or none at all. In the summer there are more English speakers around – diaspora Italians visiting the home region. Don't worry if you thought you had some Italian but still don't understand – it's the Abruzzo dialect. Speak Italian and people will switch. For a selected Italian-English glossary see Appendix C.

Note that menus are rarely translated and sometimes don't exist – the day's dishes are listed by the waiter.

But you can always manage, and unless you have a pretty restricted diet it can be fun.

MAPS

There is no comprehensive mapping of Italy for walkers. Published maps of Abruzzo are patchy, both in coverage and quality, but the maps listed in the table below are recommended and cover most walks.

The sketch maps in this guide-book should suffice for shorter walks below the tree line, but you should take the recommended sheet map as well. You should definitely take a sheet map for routes that visit peaks, ridges and open mountainside.

The recommended map for each walk is given here and also in the information box at the start of each route. A lesser alternative is given in brackets (it might not, for example, cover the whole route).

Maps can be difficult to obtain, especially outside of the region. In Sulmona, try Susilibri on Via Panfilo Manzara or the tourist information office in the Annunziata on Corso

Map	Name	Scale	Publisher
1	Majella – Carta Escursionistica	1:25,000	Parco Nazionale della Majella/ D.R.E.SM. Italia
2	Maiella National Park – Tourist Map	1:50,000	Monte Meru Editrice
3	Majella	1:25,000	Edizioni il Lupo
4	Gran Sasso d'Italia	1:25,000	Edizioni il Lupo
5	Gran Sasso d'Italia	1:25,000	Club Alpino Italiano (CAI) – Sezione dell'Aquila
6	Monti della Laga	1:25,000	Club Alpino Italiano (CAI) – Sezione di Amatrice/SER
7	Monti Marsicani	1:25,000	Edizioni il Lupo
8	Abruzzo National Park – Trekking	1:50,000	Parco Nazionale d'Abruzzo, Lazio e Molise/S.E.L.C.A.
9	Monti Marsicani – Mainarde	1:25,000	Edizioni il Lupo
10	Monte Genzana, Monte Rotella	1:25,000	Club Alpino Italiano (CAI) – Sezione di Sulmona
11	Velino-Sirente	1:25,000	Edizioni il Lupo
12	Simbruini	1:25,000	Edizioni il Lupo

Walk	Map	Walk	Map	Walk	Map	Walk	Map	Walk	Map
1	1 (3)	9	1 (3)	17	4 (5)	25	7 (8)	33	10
2	1 (3)	10	1 (3)	18	4 (5)	26	7 (8)	34	11
3	1 (3)	11	1 (3)	19	4 (5)	27	7 (8)	35	11
4	1 (3)	12	4 (5)	20	6	28	7 (8)	36	11
5	1 (3)	13	4 (5)	21	6	29	7 (8)	37	11
6	1 (3)	14	4 (5)	22	7 (8)	30	10	38	11
7	1 (3)	15	4 (5)	23	7 (8)	31	10	39	
8	1 (3)	16	4 (5)	24	9 (8)	32	10	40	12

Ovidio; in L'Aquila, try Agnelli on Corso Principe Umberto; or, near Pescara, the bookshop in the Abruzzo Centre shopping mall. Tourist information offices and park visitor centres often keep a small selection, and maps may also be found in bars, restaurants and newspaper kiosks. Keep an eye out! Maps 3, 4, 7, 9, 10, 11 and 12 can be bought online at www.edizioniillupo.it. Other suppliers include Standfords (www.stanfords.co.uk) and The Map Shop (www.themapshop.co.uk) – both of which are based in the UK but deliver by post worldwide.

ViewRanger is an online route mapping service for walkers and cyclists. Its mapping of Abruzzo is good and can be accessed via an app on a GPS-enabled smartphone when you are out and about. It can be considered a good backup to the paper map. You can create an account at https://my.viewranger.com.

USING THIS GUIDE

The 40 walks in this guide are for people who want to experience the beauty, and perhaps the challenges, of a quiet and remote part of the European upland. The routes, all of which have a grade for difficulty, vary from gentle strolls to serious expeditions in the mountains. Most start and finish in a village with a bar and shop.

About a quarter are easy-going – a half day or a relaxed full day, generally suitable for young and old alike. Averaging 7.5km in length, with modest amounts of up and down, they visit woods, gorges, lakes, hill tops and old villages.

Another quarter or so are of moderate difficulty – a full but straightforward day and not too taxing; suitable for occasional but fit walkers. Averaging 16km in length, with climbs and descents (some big but simple), they visit forests, mountainsides and some summits (one over 2000m!).

The rest, however, are long walks and mountain treks for those who enjoy a full day out. Usually about 17km in length, they involve a good climb (average 1300m), often on open mountainsides and along ridges. They visit 34 peaks over 2000m, including 11 of the region's 18 summits over 2500m. They also visit the three highest points in the Apennines. A few have one or two moves of easy scrambling and a distinct alpine feel, including one (Walk 15) that involves a section of via ferrata, for which appropriate equipment is required. Others stay lower, crossing plains and passing through woods and villages. Almost all can be shortened according to time, energy, weather and personal preference.

The route descriptions all start with a box that provides information about the walk – GPS coordinates for the start point, the likely walking time (not including rests), difficulty, distance, high and low points, total ascent and descent (often a lot more than the difference between the low and high points). Difficulty is graded as 1, 2 or 3 (1 is a straightforward wander that may involve a climb; 2 is suitable for a fit walker with reasonable experience of the hills; and 3 is for those comfortable with mountain conditions, exposure, physical demands and route finding). Several of the grade 3 walks can be made grade 2 – see route descriptions for more details. The information box also includes advice on reaching the start point, where to park and which sheet map covers the route. Additional access information is given in Appendix B.

A general flavour of the walk is provided by way of an introduction, and this is followed by a detailed route description. To aid navigation, the route description shows in **bold** places along the way that also appear on the sketch map.

GPX tracks

GPX tracks for the routes in this guidebook are available to download free at www.cicerone.co.uk/978/GPX. A GPS device is an excellent aid to navigation, but you should also carry a map and compass and know how to use them. GPX files are provided in good faith, but neither the author nor the publisher accepts responsibility for their accuracy.

ADVICE FOR THE TRAIL

Weather

Summer, even in the mountains, is usually hot, with midday temperatures commonly in the mid-30s (°C). A lot of walks are exposed to the sun, wind and possible afternoon thunderstorms. Be prepared. A weather forecast for every village in Abruzzo can be obtained from the 'Meteo' section of *La Repubblica* newspaper (www.repubblica.it). It is in Italian, but the symbols and numbers are self-explanatory.

Sheep dog and its flock

Managing the heat

Carry all your water for the day. Springs and fountains are often dry in summer. For the bigger climbs and longest routes you'll need three litres on a warm day. Keep the sun off your head. Really hot days are best avoided or made manageable with a very early start. Daybreak is a special time to begin an ascent – with a little night chill still in the air.

What to take

Take insect repellent – flies sometimes fill the sheltered, vegetated valleys. They rarely bite but can be persistently irritating. Repellent around your hat brim will help. (Bugs largely disappear above the tree line.) Don't forget a small pair of binoculars, your camera and a field guide to trees and flowers.

Especially if you are going above the tree line, take full mountain kit – strong boots and windproof hooded jacket, windproof quick-drying trousers, extra fleece, compass, whistle, map, rations and first-aid kit. Walking poles are very useful.

Sheep dogs

Sooner or later you will encounter a flock of sheep with attendant dogs. The dogs are likely to approach and bark at you (it's their job), but will essentially keep their distance. The best option is to avoid the flock if you can. If not, walk calmly and purposefully, taking a wide, skirting line without looking at the dogs. They will desist and go as soon as they realise you are leaving and not a threat. If retreat seems the best option, keep your head lowered, don't turn your back and don't run.

Rockfall and blocked paths

The mountains of Abruzzo are high, steep, forested and, in places, unstable. They are also covered in thick

33

snow in winter. Every spring there are rockfalls and avalanches, and very occasionally there may be a landslip or rockfall later in the year. Although the chances of witnessing such collapses are very small, they may affect you indirectly by bringing down trees and rubble that block paths and minor access roads. Blocked paths may remain so for a long time afterwards.

The route descriptions account for all known blockages up to the end of 2017, but others will occur in due course. Be aware of the possibility and, if you find your route barred, don't retreat straight away – it's often localised and possible to pick a way around.

Treat the mountains with respect

Thunderstorms and mists can form very quickly and are frequent on hot afternoons. Leave notice of your intended route and parking location. Remember that the Abruzzo mountains are very large, wild and empty places – treat them with care and respect.

Remember, too, that the forest is dense and extensive – stay on a good path and always know where you are.

It's easy to become disoriented, especially on cloudy days.

In the winter, snow down to 500m is common, so paths will be obliterated and rocks icy, and there are of course fewer daylight hours. Avalanches occur every year. Don't go out unless you are fit, experienced, well clothed and equipped (walking axes and snowshoes). You should start at or before dawn, know how to navigate and assess avalanche risk, and consult a good forecast. That said, a calm day with an azure sky, crystal air and sparkling snow is an amazing thing – don't be too put off!

Mountain rescue

Despite all your preparation and attention, unexpected circumstances can arise and accidents do happen. If you find that you need help, call the mountain rescue service (Soccorso Alpino) on 118. (The Italian general emergency number is 113, and the European general emergency number is 112.) It is recommended that prior to travelling you buy travel insurance that covers hill walking and mountain rescue as well as the normal travel and medical risks.

THE MAIELLA NATIONAL PARK

Monte Amaro summit cross and the Valle di Femmina Morta (Walk 9)

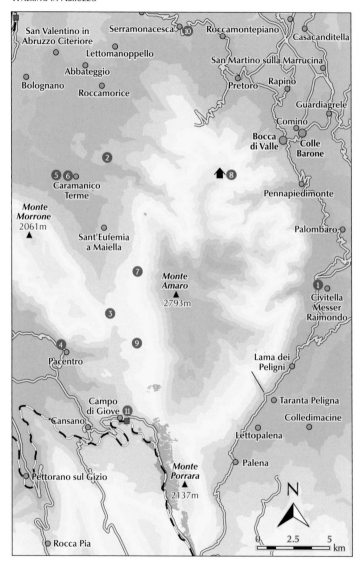

WALK 1

Fara San Martino gorge and Val Serviera

Start/finish	Car park for Fara San Martino gorge (42.087945, 14.198860)
Distance	16.5km
Total ascent/descent	2100m
Difficulty	3 (route snowbound from about November to Easter)
Walking time	7hr 30min (5hr if you retrace your steps from the high point)
High/low points	1675m/398m
Map	Majella – Carta Escursionistica (1:25,000)
Access	Fara San Martino is tucked under the steep east flank of the Maiella, at the outlet of the gorge. Reach it from the south via the SS84 along the foot of the massif through the villages of Palena and Lama dei Peligni. About 2km beyond Lama, at Corpi Santi, turn left onto the SP214 and follow signs for Fara, 4km further on. From the north, either take the SP214 from Pennapiedimonte via Palombaro or, from Guardiagrele, turn right off the SS81 at Piano Aventino, just north of Casoli, and follow signs for Fara which is 7km away.
Parking	Arriving from the south, the road descending to the village swings sharply right at a bar on the left. Turn left at this bend and follow an unsealed road, signposted 'gole', for about 150 metres to a parking area before the entrance to the gorge.

A long day out exploring two spectacular and wild gorges on the eastern flank of the Maiella massif. The village of Fara San Martino, where the route starts and ends, is a famous centre of pasta production. From there the route squeezes through the narrow entrance of the silent Santo Spirito valley, then zig-zags steeply up its north-western side to the crest, before dipping gently down the other side into the even wilder Val Serviera. The return is via the Colle Bandiera overlooking Fara, with a 3km wander along lanes to regain the start point.

The full route is demanding with a lot of ascent but highly rewarding, offering wonderful and contrasting views in the remote beauty of the national park and a good chance to see chamois and golden eagles. If you prefer not to do it all, returning through the Santo Spirito valley from the path junction, the belvedere or the high point makes a very fine day in its own right.

Walk ahead between cliffs into the tight entrance of the gorge. Squeeze through – you'll easily be able, in places, to touch both sides at once.

The eastern flank of the **Maiella massif** rises impressively above rolling hills just 25km from the Adriatic Sea. From the 2700m high, lunar-like plateau of Monte Amaro, deep gorges have been incised into

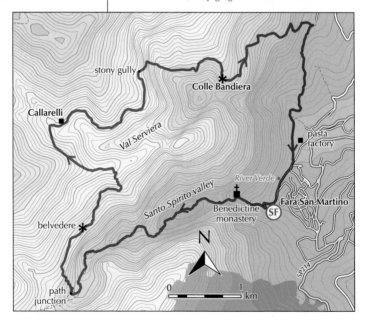

The entrance to Fara San Martino gorge

the mountainside, cutting down through the layers of limestone to form narrow, twisting, isolated worlds overlooked by dominating cliffs.

The passage opens into a secret world, enclosed on three sides – the **Santo Spirito valley**. ▸ The path leads up and into the wider gorge. Walk through the impressive valley, climbing steadily and sometimes steeply between the towering walls, for about 4km. Pass two picnic spots with fountains (often dry) and notice the changing flora as height is gained.

Towards the end the forest thickens and a **path junction** with a picnic table is reached. The left fork (do not follow this) carries on along the valley bottom, from here on called the Valle di Macchia Lunga, and eventually leads into the high mountain corrie of Valle Cannella and to Rifugio Manzini.

Instead, take the path on the right for Val Serviera. It twists steeply up through deep fallen leaves of the

The excavations in the wider gorge beyond are of an old Benedictine monastery, which gave rise to the founding of Fara.

beech forest. At half-height the path trends right, leaving the trees and continuing to a tremendous **belvedere**. Enjoy the level going and fine views down to where you recently passed. After 1km the climb recommences, with the path zig-zagging steeply up to the left. ◀ Trudge on and up to reach the crest between the valleys.

A small deviation leads to a fountain 30 metres away.

Turn left along the open ridge for 300 metres or so to reach the day's high point where the path slants obviously rightwards on the other side and back into trees. (Don't be tempted to go right too soon.) Descend gently into the **Val Serviera**, leaving the forest again and emerging onto a grassy promontory – a favoured haunt of a group of chamois (*camoscia*). Carefully locate the way off the far side and go down a short rocky gully to the river. Hop across on boulders and climb briefly up to a shepherds' hovel called **Callarelli**, 'restored' somewhat by the national park.

The authorities permit only experienced climbers to explore the canyon – its vertical cascades can be descended only with double abseil ropes.

From Callarelli, follow the level path east (right) which contours high across the grassy slopes and ledges of the left side of the valley. The views into the gorge are breathtaking. The valley deepens and narrows as the canyon develops. ◀ To avoid being drawn in, the path turns left to climb briefly and steeply over a wooded shoulder into the adjacent sub-valley.

From the shoulder, descend through trees to emerge at the top of a large **stony gully**. Snow can linger here throughout the spring but a little should present no difficulty. Descend the gully to the grassy pasture. The path levels and leads south east towards the cross on **Colle Bandiera**, overlooking the entrance to the Val Serviera. Shepherds' caves are prominent across the hillside. Ignoring paths to the left, walk up to the cross.

> The **panorama** is huge, with views back into the massif and across to Lago San Angelo, and hilltop villages scattered across the undulating countryside to the sea. Fara lies over 700m below.

Descend from the cross to join the path on the edge of the gorge. Follow it leftwards (don't be tempted

Val Serviera at Easter

down right – a track that leads only to more shepherds' caves). Pass a fountain and, swinging further left, begin the steady, long descent to the foot of the mountain. The good path leads north east – taking you disappointingly away from the village.

The descent is steady until, with relief, the path turns sharp right and, after a final swing northwards, turns right (east) again to continue down to end at a white 4x4 track. (If you reach a first small building before the sharp right turn, you have missed it. Retrace your steps for about 30 metres to find it.)

Turn right on the track towards Fara, about 3km away, and walk back along lanes, in places tarmacked and in others not, following occasional signposts marked 'G3'. In general, keep near to the foot of the mountain and pass behind the Di Cecco **pasta factory**, always heading towards Fara.

Rivers flowing through the gorges or springing from their mouths powered small industries in the settlements along the foot of the escarpment. In Fara San Martino the waters of the Verde river, which springs between the village and the mountain, gave rise to

41

pasta production. Several firms were established and, today, the output of the enormous De Cecco factory can be found in delicatessens around the world.

At one point walk alongside the river that flows from Val Serviera. The final stretch arrives at the bottom of **Fara San Martino**.

Turn right onto the main road, pass an old factory and fork right into a small park lying in the rising valley between the village and mountain. ◄ The source of the River Verde, springing from the foot of the mountain, makes an interesting pause. The last stretch up to the car park is on tiresome unsealed roads, but is soon over. Take a left turn to regain the track driven down at the start of the day for the easiest approach.

In the park are archaeological remains of early waterworks, mills and generators.

WALK 2

The hermitage of San Bartolomeo di Legio

Start/finish	Decontra, in the north of the Maiella National Park (42.169530, 14.028257)
Distance	5.5km
Total ascent/descent	280m
Difficulty	1 (route may be snowbound in the winter months)
Walking time	2hr 30min
High/low points	876m/684m
Map	Majella – Carta Escursionistica (1:25,000)
Access	Decontra is about 3km north east of Caramanico Terme, the main town in the central valley of the Maiella. Take the SR487 from the north or south to Caramanico. (For further details see Appendix B.)
Parking	Shortly after entering the village (just beyond 'Il Cervo' restaurant) the road swings left, passing a church on the right. After 200 metres the road turns right in a hairpin. Park here in a sensible spot. Alternatively, park near the stone well.

The small mountain village of Decontra lies high above the northern slopes of the wonderful Orfento valley, plunging deeply from the slopes of the Amaro massif. This gentle uphill stroll crosses the stony meadows and young woodlands of the northern Maiella foothills, followed by a steep descent into the narrow valley sheltering the centuries-old hermitage built almost imperceptibly into the cliffs of the far bank. The route offers fine views towards the sea and the Gran Sasso range and presents a quiet insight into the life of the people who lived here in times past. Return to Decontra by retracing your steps, admiring fine examples of Maiellan 'stone beehives' along the way.

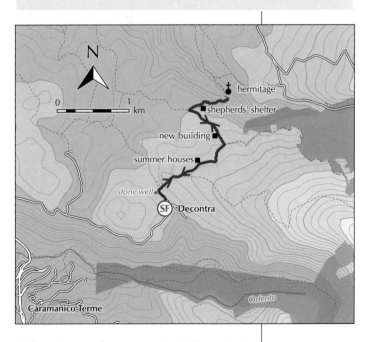

Walk north west along an unsealed white track that leaves the hairpin bend (there is likely to be a signpost for the hermitage) and in 200 metres reach a crossroads with a superb **stone well** in the field on the left.

The stone well at Decontra

Do not continue straight ahead. Instead turn right (signpost for Valle Giumentina) and, in a few metres, take the gently rising track on the right, which runs straight for about 300 metres until it reaches a larger white road. Cross over and continue in the same direction, still rising gently. Look out for red-topped posts marking the way. There are also signs for 'Eremo S. Bartolomeo'.

Pass **summer houses** to the left and right in young oak woods. In about 200 metres the track levels and, keeping to the right, passes into and through fields until it swings left across the bed of a little stream. The path becomes less evident and, leaving the larger track, heads obliquely right across meadows full of piles of rocks. Keep a lookout for the posts, which still mark the way. In a further 400 metres the path reaches another white unsealed roadway and more signs for the hermitage.

Turn left onto the white road and pass a small, **new building** on the left. In a few hundred metres a grassy track leaves the road to the right, soon passing a stone-built (slightly collapsed) 'beehive' **shepherds' shelter** (*tholos*), so characteristic of the Maiella. Continue past the shelter on the grassy track to the lip of the gorge and gaze down to the band of cliffs on the far side and the cleverly disguised hermitage itself.

> The caves and rocky walls of these remote and sheltered gorges have been exploited for centuries as havens for the pious and the persecuted. A number of **hermitages** and **small chapels** were established on the cliff faces themselves, surviving today as reminders of the region's strong spiritual past. The San Bartolomeo di Legio hermitage, hidden away in its narrow gorge, is perhaps the most accessible and interesting.

Descend steeply to the right, passing an excellent grassy picnic spot about a third of the way down. At the bottom, cross the little river by a small bridge largely comprised of very big boulders. Climb the path on the other side to arrive at the left side of the **hermitage** and the ancient steps to the terrace. Reverse the route to return to **Decontra**.

The hermitage of San Bartolomeo di Legio

WALK 3

Monte Morrone from Passo San Leonardo

Start/finish	Passo San Leonardo (1280m) – the watershed of the central valley of the Maiella (42.073324, 14.030009)
Distance	19.5km
Total ascent/descent	1370m
Difficulty	2 (route snowbound from about November to Easter; in mist consider retreating, as the complex ground around the summit can be confusing)
Walking time	6hr 30min
High/low points	2061m/1080m
Map	Majella – Carta Escursionistica (1:25,000)
Access	The pass can be reached from Campo di Giove to the south or, from the north, Caramanico Terme and the Pescara valley beyond. From Sulmona it is best to go via Campo di Giove. (For further details see Appendix B.)
Parking	At the ski lodge (Rifugio Celidonio)

The 20km Morrone chain is the western, slightly lesser half of the Maiella massif. It forms the impressive north eastern wall of the Sulmona basin, dominating the view north from the town itself, culminating in the 2061m summit of Monte Morrone, which is snowcapped for much of the year. This is a long route but reaches the summit of Monte Morrone with relative ease, following an old mule track through beautiful beech forest and then the broad ridge itself. Views across the Sulmona valley and, in the other direction, to the Monte Amaro massif are spectacular. Descent to the ancient hamlet of Roccacaramanico is steep but the route finishes with a gentle rise through the central Maiella valley.

Follow a path from the corner of an outbuilding, obliquely leftwards up the steep meadow and into the forest. ◀ The path becomes a distinct and broad mule track that soon twists upwards. There are red-and-white waymarks – the route is numbered '2' on occasional

A landmark is the top of the small ski lift just before the trees.

signposts. At a junction, about 200 metres after entering the forest, take the path on the right (signed '2' and/or 'Q3'), which continues to climb. A few hundred metres further on, the path, now running north west, forks at a **small meadow**.

The left fork rises steeply to Monte Mileto, the first peak on the Morrone chain, but take the right-hand path across the meadow and back into the forest. This is the start of a wonderful 3km passage through beech trees on the gently rising mule track. As you approach the tree line, the path steepens into a series of zig-zags to reach the junction with the route up from Roccacaramanico, a point known as **La Piscina**. Out of the trees, the path soon arrives at the **Rifugio Capoposto** shepherds' hut below the summit of Monte Le Mucchia.

The path enters the low rising valley running north west between Monte Le Mucchia to the north east and Monte Cimerone to the south west. It climbs gently along the right side before gradually drawing away from the valley bottom to reach a small saddle. At the saddle a further valley, still running north west, commences. The path runs for a further 500m before gaining a second small saddle. The summit of Morrone finally appears further ahead to the left. Rifugio Iaccio della Madonna lies ahead at the end of the elongated basin below the north east flank of the mountain.

Take the path that traverses left to gain the **saddle** between the peaks of Morrone and Cimerone. The Sulmona valley finally appears below, with the path signed '7' or 'S', from Badia/Fonte d'Amore, reaching this same point. Head up north west and quickly turn north to reach the small depression before the summit block. The path leaves the depression to climb up and onto the ridge on the right from where it follows the crest northwards and upwards, across stones and short grass, to reach the 2061m **Monte Morrone** summit in just under 1km. The views are magnificent, notably of the Monte Amaro massif across the Upper Orta valley to the east and, in the opposite direction, the Sulmona valley with the peaks of the Sirente-Velino beyond.

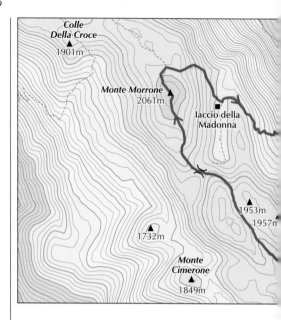

Monte Morrone is strongly associated with the medieval hermit **Pietro da Morrone**, who in 1294 was persuaded to leave his primitive dwelling on the mountainside and become the new Pope, Celestine V. He performed the role as best he could, but the cap clearly didn't fit, and just a few months after his enthronement he left the papal court to return to his simple life on the mountain. Widely condemned for dereliction of holy duty, Pietro was arrested by his successor and jailed for 'cowardice' and 'the great refusal'. He died a prisoner two years later. The church, however, soon reappraised him and in 1313 made him a saint – one of the most popular religious figures in Abruzzo to this day.

From the cross, walk about 150 metres and descend to a signpost. Turn right and follow the path over a saddle and down towards the Iaccio della Madonna rifugio

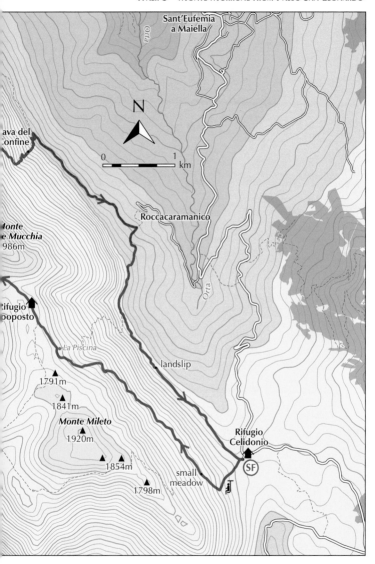

Roccacaramanico

The views across to Amaro are again wonderful.

(which should have been easily seen from the summit). The path is not well defined, so take your time to be sure of the right line. Go to the recently refurbished rifugio and imagine what life must have been like to live there...

Take a red-and-white signed path a few metres left of the rifugio that climbs out of the small valley. It soon turns right (south east) and begins a gentle descent through meadows. ◄ Once below the treeline the way continues south east, partially contouring the hillside, until the descent valley (**Rava del Confine**) is reached. From here it's steeply down, zig-zagging through the forest until, finally, the unsealed road that runs along the base of the slope is reached. Turn right (south east) and stroll the easy 2km to **Roccacaramanico**.

From this ancient village, which like many in Abruzzo is being slowly restored and revitalised, return to a point about 100 metres back towards the wooded slopes. Take the left fork to continue south east along the margin of the forest. The path levels at the trees and soon reaches another fork. The right-hand path is the steep ascent to La Piscina.

Go left and continue gently through the trees to the **landslip** – a garish 100-metre gash that has swept away the original path. Clamber down to the broken ground and take the simplest line straight across. On the far side, clamber back up and rejoin the path, which continues its shady ascent towards the ski lodge, emerging onto the meadow for the final 200 metres to **Rifugio Celidonio** and the car park.

WALK 4
Morrone di Pacentro and Monte Mileto

Start/finish	Pacentro village centre (42.050044, 13.991146)
Distance	19.5km
Total ascent/descent	1555m
Difficulty	2 (route snow-affected from about late November to May)
Walking time	7hr
High/low points	1920m/686m
Map	Majella – Carta Escursionistica (1:25,000)
Access	Pacentro is on the eastern side of the Sulmona valley; it is best reached from Sulmona on the SR487 that passes Sulmona cemetery. There is a regular bus service between Sulmona and Pacentro.
Parking	Park in the nearest allowable spot to the central Piazza Umberto 1. The bus stop is nearby.

Viewed from all corners of the Sulmona valley, the elegant 1800m peak of Morrone di Pacentro, standing prominently above Pacentro, beckons to be climbed. The mountain looks steep and challenging from the valley, but in fact it can be visited by most fit walkers. Beyond it, unseen from below, lies the 1920m Monte Mileto – a fitting climax to the day's explorations. The views from both peaks are sublime. The return to the historic village of Pacentro is via the rifugio at Passo San Leonardo and the ancient mule path that picks a lovely way above the Vella gorge.

In the summer of 2017, the first part of the route – the steep climb to Morrone di Pacentro from the village – was affected by wildfire that blackened extensive areas of grassland and burned some of the forest. Such events have always occurred from time to time and recovery is usually swift.

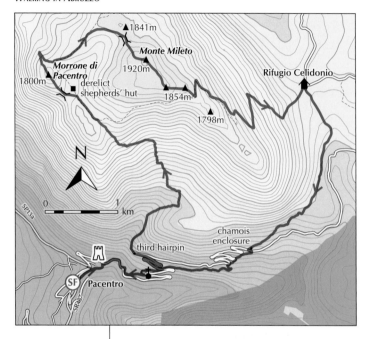

The Caffè de Martinis, in the central square of Pacentro, is a fine place to take your cappuccino and cream cake – essential fuel for what lies ahead! Start along the long cobbled street to the left of Caffè de Martinis – Via Santa Maria Maggiore – that goes through the heart of the old village. Emerge at the twin towers of the **castle** at the far end and go up to the tarmac road on the left. Walk right along the road to Ristorante La Furnicella, where a path goes left. Walk up it, behind the building, and on until it intersects the tarmac again at a hairpin just past a little **chapel**.

A few metres down the road the path leaves it again on the left. Go up the path for about 300 metres until it meets the road for a second time. Turn left and walk up the quiet road, past a picnic site on the left, and then around two hairpin bends until a longer stretch leads to a **third hairpin** where the path leaves again on the left.

Go along the path for about 50 metres to the end of a low wall on the right. Now turn right (don't continue ahead) and begin to climb a series of low rock steps until you enter the forest (the trees may still be blackened). The path climbs in a near straight line through forest for about 1km until the trees thin and you walk through clearings and glades.

Continue to climb steadily through sparse woodland until the path turns noticeably left and you ascend a steep meadow to reach thick beech woods above. The path climbs steeply through the trees via zig-zags until, a little less steeply, it contours leftwards and emerges onto open grassland. Keep climbing the pasture, rightwards, to reach a final short passage through trees and then flatter ground. Finally, the day's hardest work is over!

The path is soon joined from the right by a 4x4 track and descends into a grassy bowl with water troughs. A **derelict shepherds' hut** lies ahead but the route leaves the track and heads left to gain the obvious **saddle** on the skyline and the start of the south east ridge of Morrone di Pacentro. There is no path. The saddle affords the first sudden glimpse of the enormous view down to Sulmona. When you've got over your delight, turn right and walk up the ridge to the 1800m **summit**. ▶

The whole of the Valle Peligna is spread out below, while behind – and 120m higher – lies the open rounded top of Monte Mileto.

Continue down the north west ridge of Morrone di Pacentro (there is now a slight path) to reach a solitary small pine tree with a red-and-white paint mark. Near this point, make a sharp turn back right to follow a more

The south east ridge of Morrone di Pacentro

defined path into trees on the east flank of the peak. The path leads through the trees before regaining the 4x4 track on grassland. Turn left (north east) and walk easily along the track for about 600 metres before heading off rightwards (again, no path) to contour around the shallow valley on your right and reach the low **saddle** ahead, below the rounded north west ridge of Monte Mileto.

At the saddle, turn right and make the final climb to the 1920m **summit** cairn. There are occasional markers and a faint path to the right of the ridge. The view in every direction is spectacular – perhaps especially so to the east, across the wide meadows of Passo San Leonardo to the lonely summit of Monte Amaro, crowning the long and beautiful ridge that runs south east to Guado di Coccia.

Head south east from the summit along a broad ridge with cairns to a subsidiary peak and then, more steeply, down to the 4x4 track at a distinct bend. Step onto the track and go down it, leftwards, to a right hairpin bend. Continue along the track to reach a path leaving the track on the left. Take this path, which runs alongside the track but more directly downhill, cutting a big corner.

Below the treeline the path rejoins the track, which is then followed down through the lovely beech forest until it reaches a small meadow. In the corner of the meadow is a path junction; continue on the track, rightwards, as it makes a few final turns before reaching the bottom of the forest near an old ski lift. Go left a little and then follow the obvious path down the grass to **Rifugio Celidonio**, where refreshments await.

> The distinctive **Rifugio Celidonio** stands on the grassy saddle of Passo San Leonardo – a key point in the Maiella that not only separates the Morrone and Amaro massifs but is also the watershed of the great valley between the two. The rifugio is usually open and a most welcome place for a restorative plate of pasta or a cake. There's beer, too!

From the building, walk south east across a gently sloping meadow to the hut at the bottom of an old ski

Descending Monte Mileto at Easter

lift. The route continues in the same line along an ancient lane. ▸ Keep along this lane with occasional waymarks as it passes an odd concrete hut and then crosses more meadows before merging with a 4x4 track that arrives on the right. Walk left along the good track until it reaches the tarmac road up from Pacentro at the now abandoned **chamois enclosure** on the right.

This was once the main connection between Pacentro and the pasture of Passo San Leonardo.

Walk left for 60 metres up the road to the continuation of the path to Pacentro on the right. Go down the path, which quickly swings right and steepens, passing below the outside of two hairpin bends in the road. At the second hairpin the path reaches a 4x4 track; turn left, and then after 80 metres turn right.

The path resumes a direct line towards the village, dropping gently for 1km before reaching the tarmac once more at the spot where you turned left up the road on your ascent. Cross over the road and continue along the path, retracing your steps exactly to the cafés in the centre of **Pacentro** – where a cold beer may at this stage be more appropriate than a cappuccino!

WALK 5

The Orfento valley

Start/finish	Caramanico Terme – the main town of the central valley of the Maiella (42.157843, 14.003408)
Distance	17.5km
Total ascent/descent	1390m
Difficulty	2 (route likely to be snowbound from November to Easter)
Walking time	6hr
High/low points	1225m/521m
Map	Majella – Carta Escursionistica (1:25,000)
Access	For Caramanico Terme take the SR487, from the north or the south. (For further details see Appendix B.) There is a regular bus service from Scafa to Caramanico.
Parking	In the town centre there's a large car park and bus terminus in a hollow. Park here and walk up steps (or take the lift) to the start point. If the car park is full, find street parking (pay-and-display meters mostly).

The Orfento valley, running from the steep north west slopes of the Monte Amaro massif to Caramanico, is a magnificent place. Wild and remote, thickly forested and overlooked by massive pink-grey crags, it is strongly protected but easily accessible. A day's exploration, up the grassy meadows that flank the gorge before entering the top of the valley and returning almost its full length, is an experience long to remember. An Abruzzo gem!

The final part of the valley, through the Orfento gorge, is described separately as Walk 6. It is a natural conclusion to a tour of the whole valley, but you can return directly to the visitor centre from the San Cataldo bridge as described below.

Both routes begin and end in the centre of pretty Caramanico – a spa resort – where restaurants, small hotels and bars will fortify and refresh as you reflect on a remarkable place and journey.

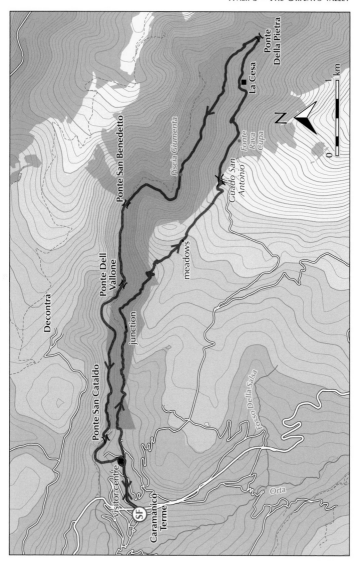

You must to check in here to be given a permit. There is no charge for this. If the centre is closed you can continue on the walk regardless. ◄

From the little piazza overlooking the car park, head east along Viale Roma with shops on the right. Pass the main spa complex on the left. In about 800 metres, the sign for the Paolo Barrasso **visitor centre** points down a lane to the left. Go into the centre and register your intent to visit the valley. ◄

> It's not by chance that the Orfento valley is such an unspoilt place: the national park and the state forestry service (Corpo Forestale dello Stato) operate a protective regime to keep it so. The **permit scheme** allows them to monitor visitor numbers; there is no general restriction on when and where you can go.

Retrace your steps to the road and turn left through the little hamlet of Santa Croce, reaching the footpaths at an information board beyond the church. The five-star La Réserve hotel is to the right; walk ahead along a level path, passing the hotel on the right and its lawned garden on the left.

The path traces the edge of the valley with the river way below to your left. ◄ Slowly the track loses height, drawing closer to the river until, almost 2km from the start, a **junction** and signpost are reached. Take the right fork for Guado San Antonio – a perfectly graded mule track which rises slightly and then contours across the valley side. At one point it crosses a smooth streambed that drops steeply to the left. Be careful – especially if it's damp.

The village of Decontra can be seen ahead on the opposite side of the valley.

The track leaves the valley by a series of zig-zags and begins to cross the rising **meadows**, full of herbs and grasshoppers, which form part of the lower slopes of Monte Rapina in the main massif. A valley runs ahead south east to meet a sealed lane (as yet unseen on the right) that comes up from Caramanico. The path climbs slowly to this point, 1.5km further on, steepening in the final ascent to the road head. This is **Guado San Antonio** – at 1225m it is the high point of the day.

Pass through the gate and descend back into the valley. The forest road winds gently down and into the head of the valley. A spring, the **Fonte Rava Cupa**, is passed in a short while. The road runs easily on for a further 1km to the new rifugio, **La Cesa**, sympathetically built by the Corpo Forestale dello Stato in a lovely clearing. ▶ A few hundred metres on from the rifugio, the path turns down left from the road to the valley floor and the **Ponte Della Pietra**. The river lies in a narrow fissure way below the bridge.

This is the turn-around point. Take the path for Caramanico along the left bank of the river (an alternative path to Caramanico lies on the right side). The going is gently undulating through the silent forest and below towering rock bluffs. After about 2km the path descends to river level. Cliffs on the left overhang the narrow path like a giant rock wave about to break. Be careful on this 100-metre section – the path is tight against the rock wall with a steep drop on the right. A section of handhold has been attached. Once through the narrows (**Piscia Giumenta**) the path widens before reaching a bridge, the **Ponte San Benedetto**.

Cross and continue towards Caramanico along the right bank of the river. The valley widens and the river

This peaceful picnic site is a good spot for lunch.

The Orfento valley in early spring

broadens. The path runs gently alongside for a further 3km, mostly through beautiful beech trees but with open sections across the bottom of rocky slopes. Along the way a side path leads up to Decontra and a second bridge appears – a rickety construction called the **Ponte Del Vallone**. Stay on the right bank and eventually cross back to the left at **Ponte San Cataldo**, just before the start of the Orfento gorge.

Begin to climb out of the valley but soon reach a path on the right, signposted for Ponte Caramanico. If you intend to complete your day with the section of valley through the gorge, go right here and follow the description in Walk 6. Otherwise continue along the main path as it climbs out of the valley. It passes an otter sanctuary and then the **visitor centre** on the right before reaching the tarmac road. From this spot retrace your steps through **Caramanico** to return to the start point.

WALK 6
Caramanico and the Orfento gorge

Start/finish	Caramanico Terme – the main town of the central valley of the Maiella (42.157843, 14.003408)
Distance	4km
Total ascent/descent	215m
Difficulty	1 (route occasionally snowbound in winter)
Walking time	2hr
High/low points	626m/515m
Map	Majella – Carta Escursionistica (1:25,000)
Access	For Caramanico Terme take the SR487, from the north or the south. (For further details see Appendix B.) There is a regular bus service from Scafa to Caramanico.
Parking	In the town centre there's a large car park and bus terminus in a hollow. Park here and walk up steps (or take the lift) to the start point. If the car park is full, find street parking (pay-and-display meters mostly).

The small spa town of Caramanico Terme lies at the heart of the Maiella National Park. It is an attractive place that rewards a couple of hours spent exploring and relaxing in its refined and busy centre. Not immediately obvious is the deep and dramatic gorge, cut by the Orfento river, that lies to one side of the town. This short walk combines the two in a half-day of great interest and contrast.

Initially heading east past the spa complex to the edge of town, the route drops into the Orfento valley to arrive at the beginning of the gorge. It then turns west through the narrow cleft with its overhanging rock walls – a spectacular place. After zig-zagging up and out onto the bridge that spans the gorge, the route returns to the centre of Caramanico where refreshment is in no short supply.

CARAMANICO TERME

Caramanico feels like the capital of the Maiella, situated as it is in the central depression between the Morrone chain to the west and the dominating bulk of Monte Amaro and its many sub-peaks to the south east. The well-kept little town is the main settlement of the area and has the relaxed feel of a mountain-air resort, its inhabitants comprising farming, artisan and trading families, with just enough holidaying visitors to be noticeable.

It's a charming place whose old centre is spared the passing traffic thanks to recently built tunnels. Lying at 650m, the views – especially to the north and the west – are grand, but it's not high enough to feel the cold until late in the year. The suffix 'Terme' tells you that the resort grew up as a place to take the waters, and on some corners you will catch the sulphurous smell of the mineral springs. The town's many hotels serve the spa complex, the finest of which is the luxurious La Réserve, with its own pools and treatment centres.

From the little piazza overlooking the car park, head north east and then east along the level Viale Roma with shops on the right and pass the main spa complex on the left. You may notice signs for Santa Croce or Corpo Forestale dello Stato. ▸ In about 800 metres the **visitor centre** sign points down a side lane to the left – it's necessary to check in here and get a permit.

Alternative parking spots may be found along this stretch.

61

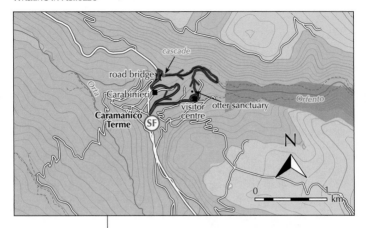

The **museum and visitor centre** is run by the Italian Forestry Commission (Corpo Forestale dello Stato). You must call in here to register before entering the Orfento valley or gorge. There is no charge, and no restriction on when and where you can go. If the centre is closed you can continue on the walk regardless.

When you have absorbed as much information as you feel you need on the remarkable local natural history, return to the main road and turn left to pass through the little hamlet of Santa Croce. Reach the start of the footpath at an information board on the left behind the visitor centre. Leave the tarmac and begin descending into the Orfento valley, passing on the left an **otter sanctuary** with its curious fence. The route is now a well-graded mule track that contours down in a rightward arc.

As you near the valley bottom there is a path on the left, signposted for Ponte Caramanico. Take this side path, down steps, to gain the **Orfento river**. The well constructed way turns left, downstream, into the narrowest part of the gorge, crossing from one side to the other on good footbridges. The walls draw in and become spectacular overhanging cliffs.

It's a secluded, **atmospheric place** where it's easy to forget you are still so close to the bars and hotels above. Notice the constructions where water is diverted into a narrow manmade runnel for irrigation and other uses.

Continue through the gorge, and after passing a cascade that plunges practically the whole depth of the left-hand wall of the canyon, you will find yourself almost beneath the **road bridge** (the Ponte Caramanico) arching overhead. The path turns to the right and commences the steep climb up onto the bridge. It's well zig-zagged and the climb will pass reasonably quickly. Turn left and cross the bridge, keeping to the left. The pavement

The Orfento gorge

Early-autumn cyclamen in the Orfento gorge

unfortunately disappears, leaving you in the road, which can be busy. Take care and soon reach a roundabout.

Take the road left, passing the **carabinieri** building, for the return to the town centre. There is still no pavement and it's a rather uninspiring end to the circuit, but it's over fairly quickly. At the next roundabout/junction go straight ahead (left). The still-climbing road swings to the right and begins to level and straighten.

A footpath appears, as do the enticing bars, cafés and restaurants of **Caramanico Terme**. Continue for a few hundred metres before finding yourself back at the start point above the car park. If time permits, wander on and explore the other parts of the attractive historical centre.

WALK 7

Monte Amaro from Lama Biancha

Start/finish	Lama Biancha road head 3km southeast of the village of Sant'Eufemia a Maiella (42.100256, 14.059335)
Distance	8.5km
Total ascent/descent	1315m
Difficulty	3 (route probably snowbound from November to May)
Walking time	6hr 30min
High/low points	2793m/1504m
Map	Majella – Carta Escursionistica (1:25,000)
Access	The beech forest of Lama Biancha is in the upper Orta valley, on the western slopes of the Amaro massif, just 3km north west of the summit. The area is reached by a side road off the SR487 between Passo San Leonardo and Caramanico. Go north 3km from Passo San Leonardo and turn off right (signposted Lama Biancha). Drive up the narrow winding lane, across meadows, then through forest to the road head. The lane is in poor condition – be careful to avoid potholes. (See Appendix B, Walk 3 for how to reach Passo San Leonardo and Caramanico.)
Parking	On a flat area almost at the tree line and directly below the ravine (Rava del Ferro)

At nearly 2800m, Monte Amaro ('the Mother Mountain') is the second highest point in the Apennines. The roof of the Maiella massif – a lonely, wild and exposed dome, snow-covered for eight months of the year – is an immense spot from which to gaze over most of Abruzzo. From a day walker's point of view, Amaro is problematic. There is no obvious circular route. You must either reverse your ascent, or traverse the mountain with the logistical problems of finishing on the other side. This guide presents three contrasting routes to the summit that could be linked as a traverse or walked as individual 'up-and-downs', depending on where you are based and the type of walk you desire.

The following route is almost the shortest (and steepest!) way to the top. From the end of the rough lane at Lama Biancha, a rocky ravine – the Rava del Ferro – rises steeply without a break and in a fairly straight line to the summit block. From the top of the ravine, the path turns right to complete the last quarter of the route across barren stones, often around snow patches, to the summit. Choose your day carefully – conditions can change rapidly, and the lunar landscape on top can be disorientating. A 6am start is advisable.

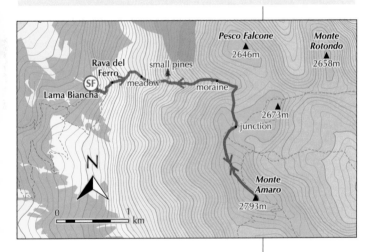

From the parking spot, go up the path to the right of the main ravine of the **Rava del Ferro**, initially through the edge of the forest. Soon reach a T-junction. Turn left and

Note the red iron
staining on the rocks
that gives rise to
the ravine's name.

climb to a grassy shoulder looking over the ravine and cliffs on the far side. ◄ The path drops to the centre of the gully where a turn right positions you for the long haul to the top. The first section, up steep, loose scree, is unpleasant, but as you approach the gap in the bluffs above, things improve. Follow the path, and occasional paint marks, carefully through the gap.

A swing right heralds the grassy second section. Continue up through the **meadow** until rocks impinge on the left and the greenery diminishes. The path clips the left side of the ravine and swings slightly to the left. Engage bottom gear and grind slowly up towards the small pines way above on the left.

> The ravine exhibits a fascinating change of **floral zone** as height is gained – from the thick beech forest, long grasses and tall flowers at the base to the hard, matted mosses and creeping alpines surprisingly clinging to the summit ground.

The earlier in the day
this section is done
the better, as it will be
in shade, with a night
cool still in the air.

There are few navigational issues to contend with – get in the groove and stay there as the valley bottom slowly diminishes and an ever-widening western horizon opens up. Rocks start to dominate underfoot. The cliffs on the right feel like the ramparts of the summit block. Watch for chamois flitting across them. ◄

Pass through or to the right of the band of **small pines** and onto the central **moraine** of a long-gone glacier. The angle eases, even flattens, along the moraine. Snow will probably be lying in the depression between the moraine and the blank flank of Monte Pesco Falcone. The path swings right and climbs southwards out of the ravine. You can sense the plateau arriving.

> The **high plateau** is a complicated area of ridges, grey crunchy peaks, isolated tops and fields of sharp, ice-cracked stones matted together by creeping vegetation. Magnificent valleys, scoured by long-gone glaciers, fall to the north and east in a series of deep, forested canyons.

The summit of Monte Amaro

Follow occasional markers and cairns carefully, always climbing southwards and probably around patches of old snow. When the ground flattens and the view opens, reach a **junction** with paths arriving on the left from Blockhaus and Monte Pesco Falcone. The unseen Rifugio Manzini lies to the east, in the corrie below the ridge.

Turn right and follow the well-marked path first south west and then, as it swings south, up and along the ridge to the summit of **Monte Amaro** with its cross and pillar. The stark, rust-red igloo of the Pelino bivouac sits a few metres away – it has been a lifesaver and will be again. Some choose to stay voluntarily, and a night on the bare mountaintop certainly has a magic of its own. Imagine the mid-summer sun rising from beyond the Adriatic.

With clear skies you can see halfway across the peninsular. The view west in particular is wonderful – down to Passo San Leonardo, across to the Morrone chain, down again to the Sulmona valley and beyond to the stilted A25 motorway, the wind farm above and the Sirente-Velino peaks in the distance.

Reverse the route exactly to descend, enjoying the beautiful view to the Grand Sasso to the north west and the Sirente-Velino to the west, and eventually returning to the start point at the **Lama Biancha** road head.

WALK 8

Monte Amaro from La Maielletta

Start/finish	Rifugio Pomilio at La Maielletta ski resort on the eastern slopes of the Maiella massif (42.160961, 14.132799)
Distance	24.5km
Total ascent/descent	1700m
Difficulty	3 (route probably snowbound from November to May)
Walking time	8hr 30min
High/low points	2793m/1881m
Map	Majella – Carta Escursionistica (1:25,000)
Access	La Maielletta can be reached from the villages of Roccamorice and Lettomanopello, both to the north, and from Pretoro to the east. (For further details see Appendix B.)
Parking	Suitable spots before the gate at Rifugio Pomilio

This is the 'via normale' from the north to the summit of 2793m Monte Amaro ('the Mother Mountain') – the second highest point in the Apennines. The best one-day exploration of the massif, it is markedly different from the steep way up from Lama Biancha (see Walk 7). Starting high, it threads a way along complicated ridges to the summit, traversing I Tre Portoni (the three saddles at the head of the Orfento valley) and offering spectacular views in all directions. Another memorable Abruzzo classic! (Descent is only by the same route or a traverse to Lama Bianca or to Fonte Romana/Campo di Giove– but revisiting those views is no real hardship.)

From the gate, walk directly up the grassy slope to the tops of the ski lifts, passing the mast complex on your left. Continue briefly along the sealed road before cutting a

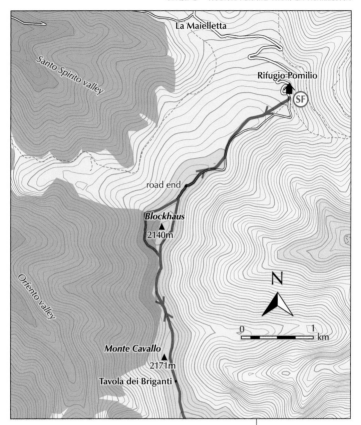

further corner by taking to the path on the right across the grass. Rejoin the road for a final time just before the **road end**, 2km from the car park.

map continues on page 71

A concrete track leads a further 100 metres to the start of the paths, by a small roofed statue of the Madonna. The remains of the Blockhaus garrison are on the hill-top directly ahead. Paths lead either side of **Blockhaus**; the one to the right is easier, skirting the hill to gain the mugo pine-covered crest behind. The views here are to the right, into the Santo Spirito valley and, further ahead, the Orfento valley.

Stroll along very pleasantly just left of the crest, bypassing the summit of **Monte Cavallo**. ◄ Descend gently to the saddle below the north ridge of Monte Focalone, passing the last fountain of the day.

> Halfway between Monte Cavallo and the saddle, the interesting **Tavola dei Briganti** can be found to the right, on the crest itself – an area of rock that bears the scratched graffiti of shepherds and 'brigands' of past centuries. This is an interesting social history, with maverick contemporary comments about the 1860 reunification among the names and initials.

The abraided path heads up the ridge, with alternative trails through the mugo. Keep reasonably to the right but be careful of the developing cliff edge. A direct line to the summit is eschewed – the path instead slants up left, climbing to the left-hand skyline via a rock ledge below a small overhang.

On the ridge a path leads left for an optional visit to the yellow **Fusco bivouac** 50 metres away, perched

The views are stupendous, with grassy slopes plunging into forested canyons.

Monte Focalone from Blockhaus

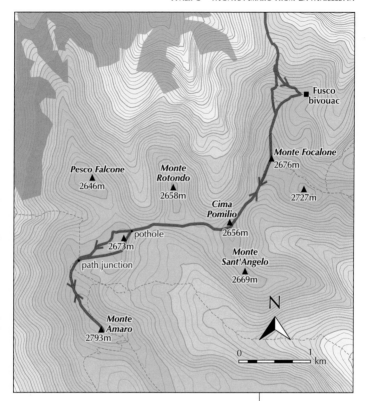

strategically on a shoulder overlooking the Murelle amphitheatre. The main route, however, turns right (south west) on the broad ridge and climbs an indistinct path to a level area where it becomes more obvious and swings left (south) to complete the ascent of 2676m **Monte Focalone**. Views of the Tre Portoni and still-distant Monte Amaro appear to the right.

The outlying Monte Aquaviva, the second highest point of the Maiella, lies east from the summit of Focalone. However, the route to follow descends south west to the first of three saddles (the Tre Portoni). ▶ Quickly reascend

Spectacular valleys fall away on both sides of the narrow ridge.

71

Fusco bivouac

to a point just behind the summit of **Cima Pomilio** and then go down again, trending right (west) to the second saddle. Monte Rotondo lies ahead and to the right, protruding into the upper Orfento valley. Walkers will be relieved that the path cuts a level track behind Rotondo direct to the third saddle. From there climb the left side of the rib, steepening significantly to pick a way through the rock band at the top.

> Where the path steepens, note the entrance to a **deep pothole** (with rope hangers above). Apparently cavers can descend over 250m, but don't lean too far!

On level ground above the rock band, head south west, following reasonable markers, over a small knoll and onto the shallow saddle and **path junction** before the summit mound. Follow the well-marked path first south west and then, as it swings left, southwards up and along the ridge to the summit of **Monte Amaro** (2793m) with its cross and pillar.

Reverse the route to descend, enjoying wonderful views in the afternoon light. There are two minor variations available. Firstly, from the **path junction** below the Amaro summit block, rather than trending left to the top of the steep rock band, follow markers straight ahead to the edge and drop to the base of the rock band. The narrow path contours tightly along the base of the cliff, with steep ground on the right, to rejoin the ascent route at the **pothole**.

For the second variation, on the descent from Focalone, continue on an obvious path down the main ridge rather than turning right towards the Fusco hut. The alternative path then turns to the right to pass above the large cliffs overlooking the Orfento valley. The ascent path is rejoined as the Mugo closes in.

WALK 9

Monte Amaro from Fonte Romana

Start/finish	At a gate 1.4km along the road north from Fonte Romana (42.054157, 14.052770)
Distance	22.5km
Total ascent/descent	1655m
Difficulty	3 (route probably snowbound from November to May)
Walking time	8hr
High/low points	2793m/1240m
Map	Majella – Carta Escursionistica (1:25,000)
Access	From the south and the west (Sulmona valley), the walk is approached via Campo di Giove. Drive from the village towards Passo San Leonardo and reach the lane to Fonte Romana after 7.3km. Continue for 1.4km to reach the gate on the right with signs and the path leading across the meadow. From the north and east, approach over Passo San Leonardo on the SR487 from Scafa via Caramanico. The gate, on the left, is 1km further along the road to Campo di Giove from the junction with the road down to Pacentro.
Parking	On the verge by the roadside. (You could park at Fonte Romana and walk the stretch along the road at the outset if you know you will descend to Fonte Romana at the end of the day – see below.)

The route from Fonte Romana – the historic way from the south west – up to the 2793m summit of Monte Amaro ('the Mother Mountain') is at least as good as Walk 8 but very different in character. It begins over 600m lower but has less overall ascent – a steady climb from meadows through the wonderful beech forest and into the great amphitheatre of Fondo di Maiella, before a long and atmospheric traverse of the Valle di Femmina Morta that leads to the summit.

While many walkers choose simply to retrace their steps from the top – the recommended option if legs are tired – two more descent variations are described here. The first requires strong boots and ankles (and hiking poles are a great help), while the second has the advantage of possible refreshment at the much-appreciated café at Fonte Romana, usually open in the summer.

From the gate, follow a good 4x4 track south east across level grass towards the trees of the extensive beech forest that covers the slopes ahead of you to two-thirds height. The well-marked path leads up into the forest, crossing at one point a forest road. From here the way steepens but remains a steady plod, mercifully shaded from the sun.

The zig-zags continue until, with a final steeper push, you emerge onto more level ground and the welcome **Fonte dell' Orso** – a trickle at the best of times and probably dry in the summer. The path crosses the ground below the foot of the amphitheatre. ◄ Climb up onto a grassy terminal moraine where the path turns left to begin its entrance into the corrie. The remains of an old rifugio suggest buildings don't last long here!

Tree debris is evidence of the avalanches that occur here every winter.

The way climbs rightwards, over grass, to join the path that ascends from Campo di Giove – passing and noting en route the junction with the path that ascends from Fonte Romana. Turn left when the Campo di Giove path is reached and begin the haul into the **Fondo di Maiella**. The track is good and follows an efficient line to the back of the corrie before turning right and climbing by way of zig-zags to a prominent rock outcrop, and from there shortly afterwards to the lip and level ground. This is the **Forchetta di Maiella**.

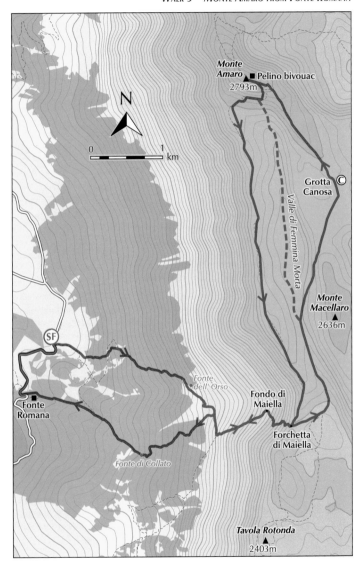

The Forchetta was a **stronghold of German alpine troops** in the winter and spring of 1944. The hollow of their gun emplacement lies just back from the edge, and the landing point of their cableway, which swung supplies up from Fonte Romana, is the rock platform that was hacked into the lip of the amphitheatre 40 metres north of where the path reaches the top.

The view is delightful. You'll return here later and, if so interested, can look for the wartime sites then if not now.

Follow the obvious path north east, which then swings left into the low **Valle di Femmina Morta** (apparently nothing to do with a dead woman, despite the name). As you turn, catch a first glimpse of the summit block that will beckon you forward for the next 1hr 30min or so, becoming a little bigger with each step.

This could be a useful shelter if conditions deteriorate, and is a traditional spot to spend a starry summer night. The view at dawn is unforgettable.

The path rises to the right to quit the valley bottom and steps up over two small rock bands before levelling out to cross the wilderness to the rocky bluff ahead. As you reach it, look for the cave – **Grotta Canosa** – in the cliff with a commanding view south east. ◀

Pass left of the cave and then cross the higher plateau, heading north westwards for 1km before the final few zig-zags begin. Turn the last bend and head for the distinctive red metal dome of the **Pelino bivouac**, standing a few metres below the cross on **Monte Amaro**'s 2793m summit.

The least complicated and probably the least energetic way down is to reverse your steps precisely all the way back to the start. This is recommended if you are feeling fatigued, as the alternatives involve, initially, a steep descent on the loose screeslopes of the summit block to arrive at the head of the Valle di Femmina Morta (this route is also largely pathless so should not be attempted in poor visibility); and secondly, a slightly longer route from the bottom of the Fondo di Maiella back to the start via Fonte Romana.

Monte Amaro summit and the Pelino bivouac

For the first alternative (steep) route, from the summit, walk back almost to the final ascent zig-zags and then descend the slope on your right (south) directly, taking good care. At the bottom of the scree you can either continue down the centre of the valley or head to the right (west) to gain the skyline crest, which is then followed leftwards, turning subsidiary tops on the left as you see fit, to reach the **Forchetta** in about 1hr 45min. Descend into the Fondo by the way you climbed earlier.

For the second alternative on the return, at the bottom of the Fondo go left at the junction with the path that descends to Fonte Romana. It's about 1.5km longer to go via Fonte Romana but the lovely path adds interest and the opportunity for refreshment at the historic and welcoming café at its end. You'll also pass another fountain halfway down – **Fonte di Collato**.

From the café at **Fonte Romana**, continue on the right to take a short but faint path direct to the road, where you turn right for the 1.3km of tarmac back to the starting gate.

WALK 10

The Alento valley above Serramonacesca

Start/finish	Centre of Serramonacesca (42.249189, 14.093073)
Distance	9.5km
Total ascent/descent	430m
Difficulty	1 (route may be snow-affected in winter)
Walking time	3hr 30min
High/low points	580m/275m
Map	Majella – Carta Escursionistica (1:25,000)
Access	Serramonacesca is best approached from the SS5, known as the Tiburtina, which runs through the Pescara valley to the north. When coming from the west, turn right off the SS5, just before Letto Manoppello, onto the SP539 for Manoppello. At Manoppello the road bypasses the little town centre to continue on and up, via many bends, for a further 4km to Serramonacesca. It is also possible to reach the village from Guardiagrele, via Pretoro, to the south east.
Parking	At the nearest allowable place to the village centre

There is far more to the Maiella than high mountain ridges and isolated peaks. The route described here is a perfect low-level, relatively short exploration of rolling hills and a shady valley on the edge of the national park, taking in the marvellous antiquities of the Abbazia San Liberatore and the Torre di Polegro.

The first section is a gently rising kilometre on a quiet road which becomes steeper before the tarmac runs out, turning into an unsealed lane that climbs though silent woodland. The track wanders gently and moves from woodland into open fields before reaching the high point of the day. From there it's a gentle downhill to the obvious and alluring remains of the Torre di Peligro, and then through wooded slopes into the valley and its good riverside path, which leads to the abbey with a seasonal café. From here the route heads easily back to the village centre – a fitting end to a relaxing day.

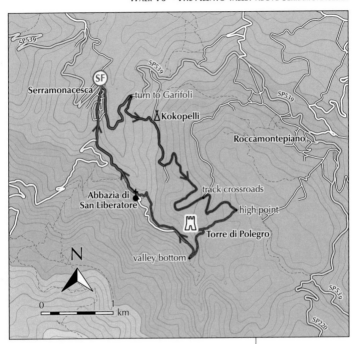

The centre of **Serramonacesca** is the junction of three roads – one up from Manoppello, another down from the Abbazia di San Liberatore and the third out to Roccamontepiano. Walk south east along the level road towards Roccamontepiano, which is followed past the church and Bar dello Sport on the left until the village houses end.

Continue along the road, crossing the bridge over the Alento, then swing left and walk 500 metres to the **turn to Garifoli** on the right. Go right steeply up the lane for about 600 metres, through meadows and olive groves, to reach the end of the steepest section and the **Kokopelli campsite**. ▶ Go right behind the campsite, past houses, for a further 700 metres. The lane now swings left, through woods, to arrive at the final house on the right.

This site is highly recommended if you are in the area with your tent or small camper van.

An old road sign marks the transition from tarmac to earth and stones.

Continue along the unsealed lane through woods to where 4x4 tracks go steeply uphill ahead (left). Go right on the main track, now rutted, and back into woods. The track makes a large U-turn to the left and climbs steadily, with views appearing south towards Passo Lanciano above the treeline. Then views appear to the north

Torre di Polegro

– across the broad valley of the Pescara river and into the distant Gran Sasso mountains.

Continue ahead, passing a **track crossroads** and below powerlines. A fork is reached in a few further metres – stay right and follow the rising rutted path, again below powerlines, as it traces a large 'Z' to arrive at a signpost at the **high point**. (At one point the path diverts briefly to the right to pass a blockage in the original way.)

The signpost indicates the path to Torre di Polegro (D3). Turn right and walk towards the ruins, which you can see in the woods ahead. Just before the tower, at an ancient shepherds' shelter in a cave, the path goes steeply down left. Take a few minutes, though, to visit the **tower**.

> The **Polegro tower** was built on a prominent rocky bluff to protect the San Liberatore abbey. Today it is a ruin but the sense of strength and impregnability pervades. It's a beautiful spot with splendid views up the thickly forested Alento gorge to the open mountainside of the Maielletta, its communication masts prominent on the skyline. Steep cliffs below lend the tower its defensive strength – be careful not to lean too far over!

Return to the cave and follow signs down the path to the **valley bottom**, arriving about 400 metres upstream of the tower.

Turn right and follow the excellent track downstream on the right bank of the torrent. Signs for Abbazia di San Liberatore (D3) will assure you all is going well. The good track crosses the river to go up leftwards towards the abbey, but stay in the gorge, on a path alongside the water, mostly on the right bank but occasionally crossing rickety bridges to the other side and back. It might be tricky in winter but otherwise the going should be fine.

> As you descend, notice the curious rock ledges carved into cliffs on the right. These are **burial chambers** that were created over the centuries by the monks from the abbey.

Serramonacesca village centre

This spot is one end of the long-distance Spirit Trail that runs across the Northern Maiella to the Abbazia di Santo Spirito in the Sulmona valley.

The waters of the Alento tumble on, pouring over small ledges into cool pools and sluicing through runnels – watch out for slipperiness! The path crosses back to the left a final time and up a steep bank to emerge, wonderfully, onto the lawn where the striking **Abbazia di San Liberatore** sits. Take your time to enjoy the peace, possibly taking a view inside and a drink at the seasonal café. ◄

The valley attracted Benedictine monks who first established the **Abbey of San Liberatore** in the ninth century, just a few kilometres above Serramonacesca on a small plateau overlooking the river. It's a harmonious place and the church is a real jewel in the Abruzzo crown.

Return to the village by way of the quiet road that leads north west from the abbey gates. Soon pass a sports field on the right and then caves and tombs carved into cliffs on the left. Staying right, descend more steeply back to the houses of **Serramonacesca**, and then the central square with its little shop and bar (not open at lunchtime – thus the tranquility of rural Abruzzo!).

WALK 11

Monte Porrara ridge

Start	Palena railway station – a 15min drive south east from Campo di Giove (41.918834, 14.105489)
Finish	Centre of Campo di Giove
Distance	14.5km
Total ascent	1045m
Total descent	1235m
Difficulty	3 (route probably snowbound from November to April)
Walking time	6hr 30min
High/low points	2137m/1067m
Map	Majella – Carta Escursionistica (1:25,000)
Access	Campo di Giove is about 12km south east of Sulmona. Palena station stands in stark isolation at the junction of the roads from Roccaraso and from the village of Palena itself, some 9km to the north east. (For further details see Appendix B.) There is a regular bus service between Sulmona and Campo di Giove.
Parking	Centre of Campo di Giove (assuming transport to Palena station has been arranged), but it will depend on your logistical plans – see below. If you leave a car at the start of the route it could be parked at the small pull-in 750 metres north east of Palena station – see also below.

This is one of the finest ridges in Abruzzo – sharp, long and high with little undulation to disturb the wonderful walk from the mountaintop. The climbs are on pleasant paths and old mule tracks through fine beech forest. The view west is dominated by a typical Abruzzese high plain, the *altopiano* Quarto Santa Chiara. East and north east lie the massive flank of the Maiella massif and the Adriatic Sea.

This walk was originally published when there was a regular service on the mountain railway that links Sulmona with Castel di Sangro and Isernia to the south. The line, the highest in peninsular Italy, cuts through the southern part of the Maiella giving perfect access to walking country. However, in

2011 the service was withdrawn (although the track remains in working order and is often used for tourist specials). The description is retained in this edition as the walk is first class and can be achieved by groups with two cars or by getting a lift or taking a taxi to Palena station. There are taxi firms in Sulmona and Roccaraso, located via the internet. And walkers may well be able to hitch a lift from Campo di Giove to Palena station too – just not guaranteed!

Note that afternoon mists are common and will make route-finding difficult. An early start is recommended.

The Quarto Santa Chiara presents a fine view to your left.

From **Palena station** walk north east along the road towards Campo di Giove. ◄ Pass over the railway tunnel entrance and continue to the point just before where the road passes over the far end of the tunnel – about 750 metres from the station. There is a small **pull-in** on the left. The obvious path slants up into trees on the right. A post marks the spot. Beware a lesser path (marked with faint red paint) about 150 metres before the correct one.

Summit of Monte Porrara

Gradually ascend the forested slope, heading north. The lower ridge is quickly gained; the trees open out into a lovely area of mixed woods and grass. Follow the rising

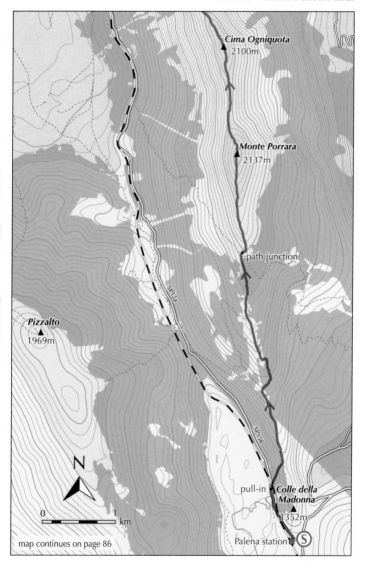

map continues on page 86

85

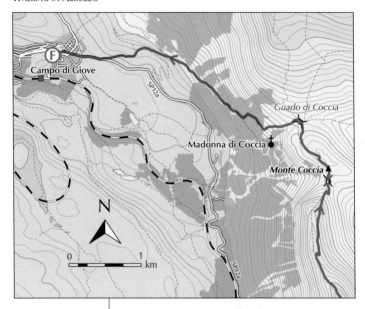

The wonderful panorama of the high plains, peaks and ridges of southern Abruzzo begins to open up.

ridge northwards, staying on it or just to its right, through open woodland and across meadow before re-entering the beech woods. About 2.5km along the ridge, reach a **path junction** where a route arrives on the right, having climbed the east side of the mountain. ◄

Climb out of the trees for the last time and onto the bare ridge. The path enters a small basin to the left that marks the start of the summit block. Regain the now obvious ridge and follow it to the 2137m **Monte Porrara** summit 1km further on. A false summit will frustrate you, but the real thing arrives quickly enough.

The view north of the main Maiella massifs – Morrone to the left and Amaro to the right – is a constant delight.

Having admired the views in all directions, follow the knife-edge ridge northwards for about 3km. The going is reasonably level, but a few sub-summits require a little ascent and descent, including **Cima Ogniquota** (2100m) about halfway along. Height is gradually lost as the village of Campo di Giove away down to the north west draws closer. ◄

86

The path eventually quits the ridge to avoid steep cliffs at its end. It drops to the right (east), zig-zagging down almost to the tree line and then runs north again, along the east flank, to a final drop into the **saddle** between Porrara and the small Monte Coccia. Be careful not to miss the descent from the ridge or you will find yourself at the cliff edge.

Afternoon mist on the crest of Monte Porrara

The path climbs out of the saddle, northwards, onto **Monte Coccia**. Turn left at the top of the button ski lift to follow the piste, past safety nets and then right, down to a second saddle, the **Guado di Coccia**, and ski infrastructure.

From the Guado di Coccia, turn left (west) to descend the piste. In about 200 metres a path develops, drawing slowly away rightwards. When the piste swings sharp left and steepens, the path continues ahead into the woods. It soon becomes a fine mule track that picks a wonderful way down through the forest and rocky bands. ◀ A path joining from the left is soon reached; the side path leads to the isolated shepherds' and travellers' chapel of **Madonna di Coccia**.

Continue down the main path as it heads gently towards Campo di Giove. Join a forest road rising from the left. Turn right along it, but after 30 metres descend left again. The final stretch to the road is along an unsealed track. At the road, turn right for the last 1km into **Campo di Giove**, passing the village cemetery, and continue easily to the village piazza with its refreshing fountain.

You are now on the Sentiero della Libertà – a wartime escape route from the POW camp near Sulmona.

CORNO GRANDE
AND CAMPO IMPERATORE

Rifugio Garibaldi below Corno Grande (Walk 16)

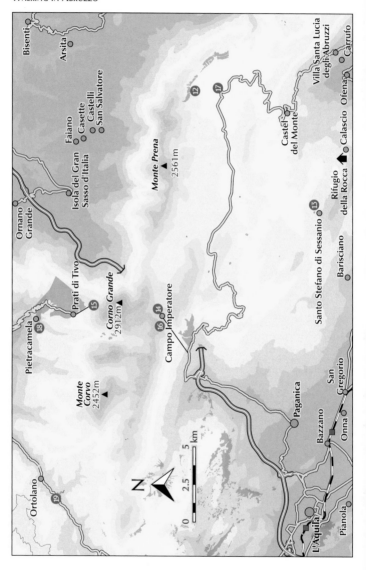

WALK 12

Monte Prena and Monte Camicia

Start/finish	Fonte Vetica – an isolated refuge on Campo Imperatore (42.424357, 13.742940)
Distance	14.5km
Total ascent/descent	1410m
Difficulty	3 (route/approach probably snowbound from October to May)
Walking time	8hr (6hr 30min if Monte Camicia is not climbed)
High/low points	2564m/1607m
Map	Gran Sasso d'Italia (Edizioni il Lupo) (1:25,000)
Access	There are two main approaches – from Castel del Monte in the south east and from Assergi in the north west. Two others might be more convenient – from Santo Stefano to the south west and Farindola to the north east. (For further details see Appendix B.)
Parking	Large car park at Fonte Vetica

This is a major excursion with an alpine feel, taking in the two main peaks of the south eastern chain of the Gran Sasso – and including a wonderful ridge walk to connect them. The views to the Adriatic are fantastic and, looking down, the huge north face of Camicia is awesome. This is a serious and memorable mountain trip. There are two places where, briefly, you need to use your hands when ascending Monte Camicia.

The route can be shortened by visiting only Prena or just the Vado di Ferruccio. In either case descent is then by retracing the climb to the Vado. Take care, start early, watch the weather and enjoy a fabulous day!

Walk back along the road from the car park and turn right up to **Rifugio Fonte Vetica**. There are no paths or way-marks for the rest of this section. From left of the rifugio, head north west (leftwards) obliquely up the grassy slope to the bottom of the Vallone di Vradda, defining the east side of Monte Camicia, just left of the trees. Cross below

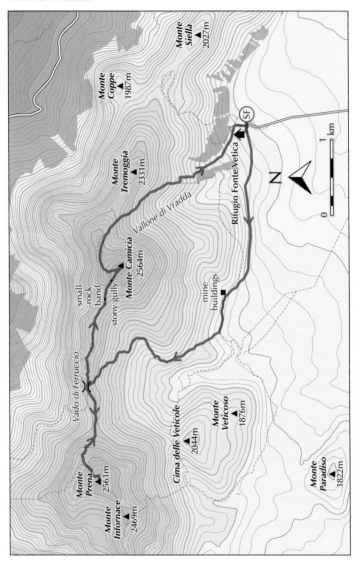

THE GRAN SASSO NATIONAL PARK

The Gran Sasso National Park is known mostly for the Corno Grande massif, the highest land in peninsular Italy. However, the park also contains the mountain chain that stretches south east from Corno Grande – a 15km ridge around 2500m, forming the north eastern wall of the Campo Imperatore high plain. The two highest points of the chain are the adjacent but marvellously contrasting Monte Prena and Monte Camicia. Prena (2561m) is a spiky, rocky mass, while Camicia (2564m) is a majestic rounded summit protected by a steep rock band.

The chain also forms the Apennine wall that rises sharply and impressively when viewed from the Adriatic coast and hill country in-between. The north wall of Camicia in particular is huge and steep. It has been called 'the Eiger of the Apennines' – an exaggeration, but you will understand the name!

retaining walls in the valley bed and go up to a water trough. Contour westwards around the base of the south-facing slopes of Camicia, staying at a constant height.

About 1km from the trough you'll intersect a large alluvial fan that spreads from the base of the mountain. Walk north west along the edge of the fan towards the old bauxite **mine buildings** a few hundred metres ahead. At the buildings, turn west (left) down the track for about 400 metres to find a waymarked path on the right, heading up a small gully.

The path climbs to a grassy shoulder from where views of the great south-facing corrie between Monte Prena and Monte Camicia open up. The shattered rocky slopes of Prena dominate the view ahead. Swing right to trace a gently climbing line around the east and then north sides of the corrie. Gullies descending from Monte Camicia are crossed – the path has been eroded in places, but no real difficulties are encountered.

The **Vado di Ferruccio**, where the path is headed, is the low point on the ridge about halfway between the two peaks. After the path swings leftwards, the Vado is soon reached. The huge views down the north wall of the chain, across the hill country of Teramo province and on to the Adriatic coast, almost 40km away, are suddenly, impressively there.

The options at the saddle are to return; to go right (east) to Monte Camicia; or to go left (west) to Monte Prena. The description to Monte Prena (and then to Monte Camicia) follows.

Walk westwards along the ridge towards the complicated steep gullies that break up the summit block. The path diverts to the right, traversing the slope for a few hundred metres before going up a shallow grassy gully to the north west ridge on the far side of the peak. From here head south west, across leveller ground, for 100 metres before turning leftwards for a steep ascent of the north west side of the upper mountain. The way is strewn with scree and loose material, but as the ridge gets closer cleaner slabs are climbed, not quite requiring a steadying hand. ◄ When **Monte Prena**'s summit ridge is gained, turn right for the cross 50 metres further on.

Take care not to lose sight of the paint marks.

The **views** from this 2561m perch are magnificent. Monte Camicia looms dauntingly 2.5km along the ridge to the south east. Vast Campo Imperatore lies like a grassy sea around the foot of the mountain. And, initially to the south west, the great spiky

The approach to Monte Prena

The summit of Monte Camicia

ridge continues to run almost all the way to Corno Grande, some 12km to the north west.

Retrace your steps to **Vado di Ferruccio**. There are two options now – return down the ascent route or continue along the ridge to Monte Camicia (it's about 2hr 30min from here to Fonte Vetica via the summit of Camicia). The weather, hour, your condition and the unavoidable small scrambles on Camicia will inform your choice. The description continues to Monte Camicia.

Head south east, following paint marks carefully. The path goes right of a high point to climb a steep, slightly loose slope. Exciting sections run along the sharp ridge before the path diverts onto the southern slope. The north side is fantastic – high, very steep and exposed. Outlying pinnacles add to the drama.

As the summit nears, the path returns to the ridge to surmount a **small rock band** with one or two hand-pulls required. Head into a **stony gully** to the right. The gully is clambered up through the ramparts, again requiring a few uses of the hands and basic scrambling moves. The

You are just 3m higher than the top of Prena and the views are just as good!

final ascent is up less steep slopes to the **Monte Camicia** summit ridge. Follow it eastwards for about 200 metres to reach the cross. ◄

Looking north, the path arching across the grassy slope of the main ridge is obvious. Return for 50 metres and then descend a rightwards-slanting path to the col above the north face. The path runs eastwards to begin a gradual descent. Keep right at a fork. Fonte Vetica lies a long way below, but the route is almost directly down, keeping left of the **Vallone di Vradda** that lies between you and Monte Camicia. The path runs down onto a shoulder and steepens through a rockier section before zig-zagging towards trees. The right bank of a small valley is followed down through bigger trees and then across grass to the car park at **Fonte Vetica**.

WALK 13
Santo Stefano and Rocca Calascio

Start/finish	Medieval village of Santo Stefano di Sessanio (42.344365, 13.642930)
Distance	10km
Total ascent/descent	440m
Difficulty	1 (route snowbound for some of the winter months)
Walking time	4hr
High/low points	1427m/1214m
Map	Gran Sasso d'Italia (Edizioni il Lupo) (1:25,000)
Access	Santo Stefano di Sessanio is situated in the Gran Sasso National Park on the south west fringe of the high plain of Campo Imperatore. It is best reached from the SS17 main road, the 'Abruzzo highway', running between L'Aquila to the north west and Popoli (and Sulmona) to the south east – approach via Barisciano. Alternatively, approach the village from Calascio or the Campo Imperatore. (For further details see Appendix B.)
Parking	Car park outside the restaurant at the west end of the historic centre

A walk between two gems of the Gran Sasso National Park and, indeed, of Abruzzo. The medieval village of Santo Stefano is being wonderfully restored and is a treat to explore. Nearby stands the castle of Rocca Calascio – an unforgettable viewpoint, sited dramatically above an ancient hamlet that is also being lovingly rescued from calamity. The route runs along a grassy ridge between the two and follows an old drove road back. Stormy summer weather should be avoided, but with suitable conditions this is a memorable half-day outing.

Following post-war mass emigration, the future of the medieval mountain village of **Santo Stefano** was uncertain. With many young people gone, the community looked set for terminal decline. Today, thanks to enthusiastic individuals and the regeneration policy of the regional government, things are different. Seventy per cent of the old buildings are restored, a number of small restaurants have opened and the population is swelled by a small but steady number of visitors. It's a lovely spot, with a powerful feel of its ancient past.

Madonna della Pietà

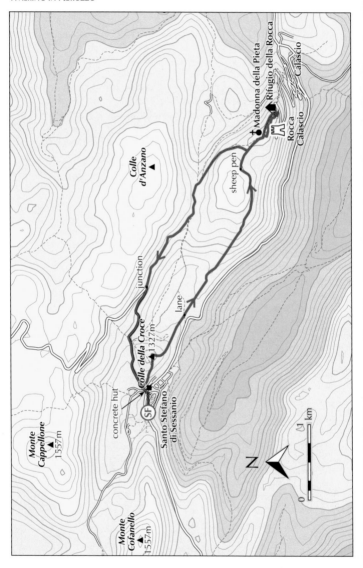

The landmark lookout tower disastrously fell during the 2009 earthquake. The rest of the village thankfully escaped major damage. A facsimile tower has been erected and the real thing will be rebuilt.

Go down the cobbled, stepped ramp on the north side of the village to the road junction. Walk 30 metres up the road that descends from Campo Imperatore to a **concrete hut** on the right. Turn right and climb the hillside on a vague path to the cross on **Colle della Croce** on the left skyline. Go on, contouring around to the right, to a rib that is descended to a **lane**. Cross over and follow a 4x4 track south east up the hill opposite. Halfway up, cross to the right of the fence and follow the waymarked path up and around the right side of the hilltop.

The views become very impressive. Keep to the level path that heads for the castle, passing an old circular stone **sheep pen** on the left. There may well be flocks here, overseen by a gang of creamy Abruzzo sheep dogs. Ignore them as best you can and they will be happy. ▶

Don't worry if the dogs bark – they're just doing their job.

The path joins a 4x4 track just before the beautiful, isolated church of **Madonna della Pietà**. From here continue along the ridge to **Rocca Calascio** and enter via the little bridge on the far side.

Rocca Calascio, at 1460m the highest fortress in Italy, dominates the valleys and villages around. Dating back 1000 years, it was badly damaged by an earthquake in 1703 but remains a forceful symbol of the power of ancient baronies. Its recent use as a film set for historical epics is easy to picture. The rampart is always accessible, and in the summer the keep is sometimes opened by enthusiastic guides.

The view from each of the four solid round towers is marvellous. Corno Grande stands massively on the northern skyline, but arguably the best vista is to the south and the Maiella massif 40km away. With luck the central keep will be open.

Santo Stefano di Sessanio

You can even stay in an atmospherically restored room.

Carry on through the ruins to drop to the half-abandoned hamlet and the welcome **Rifugio della Rocca** for a drink, panini or a full meal. ◄ The village of Calascio lies below to the south east.

From the rifugio, turn back and pick up an unsealed white road that passes below and to the right (north east) of the fortress. The level track returns to the church. Continue along the 4x4 track, descending to the right. At the junction with another white road, turn left and continue north west, mostly on the level, for 2km to reach a **junction** with the road down from Campo Imperatore.

Turn left and descend to the village along this quiet road. An occasional car will pass, so keep an eye out. You will return to below the north east side of **Santo Stefano** – ascend the ramp to the car park, from where your wander through the narrow alleyways and up and down the steps of the historic centre can begin.

WALK 14

The west summit of Corno Grande

Start/finish	Campo Imperatore hotel – the top station of the cable car (42.442641, 13.558805)
Distance	10.5km
Total ascent/descent	1080m
Difficulty	3 (route probably snowbound from October to June)
Walking time	6hr 30min
High/low points	2912m/2128m
Map	Gran Sasso d'Italia (Edizioni il Lupo) (1:25,000)
Access	The hotel is located at the north western end of the Campo Imperatore high plain. It can be accessed directly by the cable car from Fonte Cerreto, or you can drive by turning off the road that runs the length of the plain, from Assergi to Castel del Monte. The hotel lies 8km from the turn-off. (See Appendix B for details of how to reach Fonte Cerreto and the road for the hotel.)
Parking	Either at Fonte Cerreto or, if you have driven up, in the hotel parking area

This is the one mountain walkers all want to do – the 'via normale' to the highest point in peninsular Italy at just under 3000m – Corno Grande. This surprisingly straightforward route to the top, involving only a little over 800m of ascent, is quieter, more adventurous and more scenic if you take the west ridge option, with a few minor scrambling moves. The views from the rocky summit on a clear day are enormous and include the little Calderone glacier, the most southerly in Europe. See it while it's still there! Do not underestimate this mountain. It stands high and alone – a bad-weather magnet. It is likely to be misty, and thunderstorms can spring up very quickly.

A moment of Italian history took place at the **Campo Imperatore hotel**. Mussolini had been ousted from power in July 1943, arrested and brought to the Gran Sasso to be kept out of the hands of the Germans. However, it didn't last for long. On 12 September 1943 Nazi paratroopers staged a raid. They crashed their gliders into the mountainside, overpowered the guards and seized him. He was flown out in a tiny plane to German-controlled northern Italy. There are some fascinating photographs on the hotel walls, and the room where he stayed has been left as it was then.

From the car park head north, left of the botanical garden and observatory, to climb a steep, wide track. Some

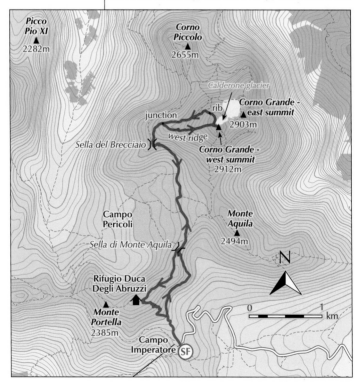

200 metres up the track a well-trod but narrower path sets off right to traverse the south eastern slopes of Monte Portella. Follow it for an easygoing 1km until it climbs steeply but swiftly to a saddle – the **Sella di Monte Aquila** – from where the view north to Corno Grande is revealed across the grassy alpine slopes of Campo Pericoli.

Turn right on a broad track along the ridge for 100 metres. At an obvious fork, turn left (north) and follow the good path across grassy slopes, gently descending towards the foot of a rocky rib, 1km away, plunging from the west ridge of Corno Grande. At the rib turn left (west) to begin a slanting ascent of the loose, scree-covered southern flank of the ridge. The going gets progressively steeper, with the final section zig-zagging up through rocks to reach the **Sella del Brecciaio**, at the foot of the west ridge.

From the Sella the path crosses to the north flank of the ridge and swings east. Further steep zig-zags are climbed over scree until an ample basin is reached. ▶ Fine views north across to Corno Piccolo appear. Just before the basin is a **junction**, with a marked path going right to the west ridge. The ridge route is recommended if you are comfortable with exposure and with using your hands for a small number of easy scrambling moves; otherwise you should follow the via normale.

The observatory at the start point

Patches of snow linger here throughout the year.

*On the west ridge
of Corno Grande*

For the ridge: Take the path on the right easily up to the west ridge. Put away your walking poles and set off leftwards (east) on a direct line up. There are paint splashes to guide you, but the path always tries to stay on the ridge itself, initially mostly on the left side and then, towards the top, on the right. The way feels like a real climb to the top and the views to either side are tremendous. All too soon the fun is over and the via normale is rejoined, arriving on the left to lead to the summit.

Alternatively, **for the via normale:** cross the basin, headed east, and gain height up a wide scree-filled track. Always stay parallel to the west ridge, which is above you to the right, avoiding paths that fork left. The path turns right just before a distinct rib dropping from the summit and climbs steeply over slabs towards the top of the west ridge. Keep following the painted circles. As the ridge is neared the path trends back rightwards (south west) and the angle eases. Just before the west ridge, step up on the left and gaze down to the small **Calderone glacier**, sitting precariously in the wild corrie below.

The path turns left (eastwards) to continue easily to the **Corno Grande west summit** (2912m – the highest of three separate summits).

> **Corno Grande**, the towering mountain of the Apennines, receives more attention than neighbouring peaks, but it can still be a lonely, magical and wild place. Seen from the south, it stands as a huge rock pyramid, rising separate and aloof above the high plain of Campo Imperatore. From the east, it crowns the long mountain wall that runs through half of the region – its seemingly impregnable north east face dominating the country to the sea.

Sign the visitors' book and prepare for attention from scavenging choughs when you break out your lunch. With luck the mist will have held off and the remarkable views can be fully savoured (although in cloud the magic of the place is perhaps even stronger). The central and east peaks stand isolated a few hundred metres away, both a more difficult prospect. Corno Piccolo, though, 1km to the north, is a story for another day…

Descend by reversing the via normale path as far as the **Sella di Monte Aquila**, from where you may continue down the ascent route directly to the car park or make a slight but worthwhile diversion for a final view and – maybe – refreshements.

To make the diversion, continue south west on a path that heads easily up and along the ridge towards **Rifugio Duca Degli Abruzzi**, which stands prominent just before the summit of Monte Portella. The path initially runs to the right of the ridge before gaining it and continuing airily to the building. ▶ The steep way down the south-facing slope is obvious. Take the path from the hut, down many hairpins, to arrive back in the car park at **Campo Imperatore**.

The historic hut is open every day from mid July until the end of September, and is also a great place to overnight.

WALK 15

The east summit of Corno Grande

Start/finish	Top of the Prati di Tivo ski lift (42.487245, 13.568294)
Distance	7km
Total ascent/descent	1060m
Difficulty	3 (route probably snowbound from October to June)
Walking time	6hr 30min
High/low points	2903m/1195m
Map	Gran Sasso d'Italia (Edizioni il Lupo) (1:25,000)
Access	Prati di Tivo is a ski resort on the north side of Corno Piccolo. Reach it by turning south up a steep side road from the SS80 that cuts east–west across the Apennine backbone, linking Teramo and L'Aquila. The turn-off lies about 7km west of the small town of Montorio al Vomano. Whether approaching from the east or west, keep a close lookout for the unassuming junction, which creeps up quickly. Follow the road for five twisting kilometres towards the village of Pietracamela. Shortly before the village, signs indicate Prati di Tivo on the left. Go left up more hairpin bends to arrive, in another 4km, at the large car park near the ski lifts.
Parking	Ski lift area car park

First, an admission – this is not entirely a hiking route. Its upper section is a via ferrata, involving the use of harness, helmet and lanyards with carabiners for the protection to be used correctly. It's not difficult in terms of moves on the rock but the exposure is enormous and exhilarating, and the east summit is a spectacular and beautiful place – all in all, a potential high point of a trip to Abruzzo.

The route, however, consists of two distinct parts. It can be enjoyed either in total or as a satisfying hike up to the Franchetti mountain hut – with further exploration if desired – and back. However you play it, it's an outstandingly beautiful route in a wild and inspirational place.

Note that the Prati di Tivo ski lift is not always running – check www. pratiditivo.it beforehand to avoid disappointment. The alternative is an additional 550m of ascent on foot from the car park to the Madonnina crest; not a welcome start to the day!

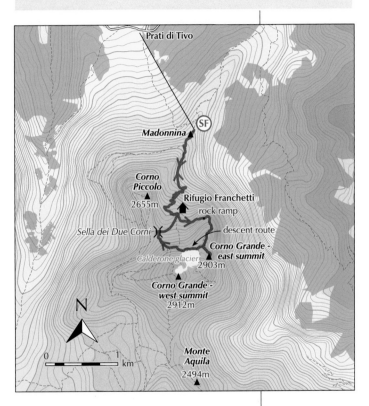

The ski gondola (or the path if you're out of luck) will deposit you on the very fine crest of the **Madonnina**. It is actually the north east ridge of Corno Piccolo, the east wall of which will loom most impressively on your right all the way to the Franchetti hut. ▶

Some people go no further than here – understandably, as the view is already magnificent.

107

Go right (south) on the very good path, following signs for Rifugio Franchetti. You will pass immediately the little statue of the Madonna (Madonnina) in her stony niche. The obvious path climbs the 400m of ascent to the rifugio on a good, well-graded surface. The gentle, green slopes are soon left behind and light grey limestone becomes dominant.

> As you progress, look and listen for climbers on the famous **rock routes** that ascend Corno Piccolo's east face; this is a historic place where Apennine rock climbing has its deepest roots.

The hut appears in view above, with its cheerfully fluttering flag, but at this stage it looks disappointingly small. However, it quickly becomes bigger as the zig-zags, first up a grassy shoulder and then through boulders, draw you closer. The final level steps take you onto **Rifugio Franchetti**'s wooden terrace, where you can take off your rucksack and enjoy the magnificent view while deciding what to do next.

WARNING

Do not attempt the via ferrata unless you have a harness, via ferrata lanyards, gloves and a helmet. You must be comfortable with easy scrambling, not tired and not overly worried by heights and exposure (reversing is awkward).

If you are not equipped for the via ferrata, you might choose to relax at the rifugio for a while before either retracing your outward route or, if you have time and energy to spare, setting off up to the saddle (Sella dei Due Corni) between Corno Piccolo and Corno Grande. From the saddle you could go left and further up the northern slopes of Corno Grande. At a path junction you could go left again on a path that heads into the wild corrie of the Calderone glacier – there's very little of it left so you might as well take the opportunity. At some point reverse your steps to the hut and then back to the Madonnina.

If you are suitably equipped, in good shape, and the weather forecast is fine (check with the warden if possible), then it's time to don your harness (it's easier here) before taking the level path across a slope, south and then east from the hut, to the bottom of the big, left-leaning **rock ramp**. The cables begin here – as does the big atmosphere. Make sure you're fully kitted up, and then set off up the ramp.

The going is glorious, the way obvious, and height is quickly gained. The ramp ends and you turn right onto an upper scree slope. To your left is, well, nothing – a huge void that is the east face of Corno Grande. Go up the easy slope without cables until they recommence to help you up a rock band. The cables are intermittent on the final slopes up to the summit block, but they are always there when you feel the need.

Approaching the top, the way is a little steeper and rockier. Keep a good eye out for paint markers, although the path is good. Pass the junction with the 'via normale' coming from the right and quickly arrive at the magical **east summit of Corno Grande** (2903m) – no cross, and probably no people.

The **views** from the summit are superb. To the west lie the central and west summits of the mountain,

Looking across to the central and west summits of Corno Grande

Corno Piccolo with the Madonnina in the sun

separated from you and from each other by deep clefts. To the north west is Corno Piccolo, now a way below; to the south is the long chain of peaks leading to Monte Camicia; and to the east is the sea.

Leave your kit on (including your helmet) for the time being and return down the upper slopes, keeping a sharp lookout for the top of the **descent route** – the via normale – especially in poor visibility. It's about 200 metres from the summit and the paint markers are good. Turn left and descend the path, westwards, steeply down to the rubble-filled **Calderone glacier** basin. Keep a good eye out for the most trod way as variations exist. In places you might want to use your hands but it's not tricky and these spots may have had cable added recently. Leave your kit on until you are well away from the slope. The middle of the moraine is a convenient place to de-harness.

The path then leads north west, with cairns and paintmarks to guide you to the top of the ridge that drops northwards to the **Sella dei Due Corni**. Go down on a clear path with the rifugio below and to the right. At the saddle, go right and easily down to the **hut**. Reverse your steps from the hut back to the **Madonnina**, hopefully in time for the last gondola.

WALK 16
Campo Pericoli and Pizzo Cefalone

Start/finish	Campo Imperatore hotel – the top station of the cable car (42.442641, 13.558805)
Distance	13km
Total ascent/descent	1205m
Difficulty	3; or 2 if omitting ascent of the two peaks. (Route probably snowbound from October to June.)
Walking time	6hr 30min
High/low points	2533m/1918m
Map	Gran Sasso d'Italia (Edizioni il Lupo) (1:25,000)
Access	The hotel is located at the north western end of the Campo Imperatore high plain. It can be accessed directly by the cable car from Fonte Cerreto, or you can drive by turning off the road that runs the length of the plain, from Assergi to Castel del Monte. The hotel lies 8km from the turn-off. (See Appendix B for details of how to reach Fonte Cerreto and the road for the hotel.)
Parking	Either at Fonte Cerreto or, if you have driven up, in the hotel parking area

A great alpine basin at the head of Val Maone in the Gran Sasso, Campo Pericoli on a summer's day seems the very opposite of the 'field of dangers' that the name suggests – a benign pasture of low grass ridges and shallow depressions traced through by a network of paths. Even more so in May when shrinking snow patches reveal a rich carpet of bright alpine flowers. But this is a high and wild place; a glacial corrie lying at 2200m, inaccessible for much of the year and surrounded by the towering peaks of the Corno Grande group and the ridges that link them.

Shortcuts are possible and are mentioned in the route description, but for anyone comfortable in the big mountains, the full route is recommended – undoubtedly the finest exploration of the basin and the wonderful mountains that enclose it.

Note that the ascent of Pizzo Cefalone involves a short section of narrow path across a steep slope, followed by a brief section of moving up through rock bands where some hand-pulls are needed – not especially challenging or exposed, but certainly a few scrambly steps rather than a walk.

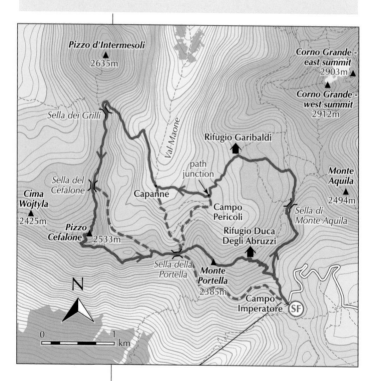

From the car park head north, left of the botanical garden and observatory, to climb a steep, wide track. Some 200 metres up the track a well-trod but narrower path sets off right to traverse the south eastern slopes of Monte Portella. Follow it for an easygoing 1km until it climbs steeply but swiftly to a saddle – the **Sella di Monte Aquila**.

Continue for 300 metres along the gently descending path from the Sella towards the west ridge of Corno Grande, then take a side path that heads left and down towards **Rifugio Garibaldi** and the heart of Campo Pericoli. There is a low sign on the right. Go down this path to the lovely old hut about 650 metres away (and initially hidden from view).

En route to the hut, the view ahead is impressive. The two prominent peaks that rise from the ridge opposite are the daunting Pizzo d'Intermesoli on the right and, one of today's goals, Pizzo Cefalone on the left. Just to the left of Pizzo d'Intermesoli and further away is Monte Corvo (Walk 19). The saddle at the base of the steep south ridge of Pizzo d'Intermesoli is the Sella dei Grilli.

Rifugio Garibaldi itself may seem a little over-engineered but has been here for 130 years. In winter it is buried in snow to the roof line! (Yes, that is a way in via the chimney…) It's a lovely spot and open for accommodation in July and August; you may be able to see inside at other times.

Leave the hut on the good path that runs south west towards Pizzo Cefalone. About 500 metres along, just before the low point where the way swings right and then begins to rise, there is a **path junction**. Turn right here and descend towards the Val Maone. (This is also the first shortcut opportunity – you could take the path that climbs to the Sella della Portella, saving 2–3hr in your day, and from there resume the route description below.)

Arrive in a further 500 metres at the head of **Val Maone** and another path junction. Turning left here also leads up to Sella della Portella (another shortcut opportunity that will save at least 2hr), but for the full route turn right down the valley and towards the close-by ruins of a building known as **Capanne**. At the ruins the path forks – go left, following red-and-yellow paint markers, to begin the climb up to Sella dei Grilli.

Approaching Rifugio Garibaldi with Pizzo d'Intermesoli behind

The path rises gently as it draws away leftwards from the path down Val Maone, but then it steepens and swings left, then right, to cross scree and boulders. The climb continues, quite steeply in places, until the path cuts across to the right to join a path up the scree from futher down Val Maone. Continue a little more easily before a final swing leftwards leads to the crest and the **Sella dei Grilli**.

> It was worth it – the **views** are special! This is the very heart of the Corno Grande massif – east is Corno Grande, north Pizzo d'Intermesoli, west the Conca Venaquaro and Monte Corvo, and south Pizzo Cefalone.

Go south on the soon-rising path towards Pizzo Cefalone, which stays just right of the crest. At one point it is narrow and a little faint as it crosses a stony slope dropping to the right; take this short section with appropriate care and soon after arrive at a nick on the crest – **Sella del Cefalone** – where there is a signpost and path junction. A third shortcut goes left from here and descends steeply from the crest on a good path below the east face of Pizzo Cefalone and directly to Sella della Portella. If you do not want to use your hands (briefly) on the ascent of Pizzo Cefalone, you must take this shortcut. Otherwise continue the steady ascent of the north ridge.

The path is now less well trod but still marked and clear. It goes up grassy, slabby slopes towards the summit block and finds the way of least resistence through the rock bands, turning right and then into a small chimney where you need to use your hands to pull a few times. The moves are easy and do not feel particularly exposed. In a few minutes you are on the 2533m summit of **Pizzo Cefalone** with its twin crosses. ▶

The views include the huge southern aspect of the massif, down across L'Aquila and into the mountains of the Sirente-Velino.

Descent is down the south face – find the marked path about 20 metres west of the crosses. It picks a zig-zag route through boulders and rock bands until, soon, you are at the top of the steep grassy slopes that rise to the summit block. The path goes left (east) and passes below crags from where a family of chamois often gaze down

Pizzo Cefalone from Sella dei Grilli

and make you feel rather clumsy. The delightfully level path runs on, contouring just below the east crest until soon arriving at **Sella della Portella**.

A final shortcut could be made here by taking the good path that goes right (south east) for a gentle descent across the open slopes direct to the Albergo Campo Imperatore. It will also save you about 1hr. However, the final climb up and along the crest to Monte Portella and Rifugio Duca Degli Abruzzi, strikingly sited on the ridge beyond, is worthwhile.

Climb steeply up from the Sella on a good path headed east. The path stays close to the edge as it approaches the low-key summit of **Monte Portella**. Pretty much all of the walk lies ranged about below; a perfect moment to reflect on the delights of the day. Refreshment may be available at the **rifugio** 300 metres beyond the summit. ◄

The steep way down the south-facing slope is obvious. Take the path from the hut, down many hairpins, to arrive back in the car park at **Campo Imperatore**.

> The historic hut is open every day from mid July until the end of September, and is also a great place to overnight.

WALK 17
Monte Bolza ridge

Start/finish	Road junction with two wooden butcher's shops in the centre of southern Campo Imperatore (42.407187, 13.744691)
Distance	14.5km
Total ascent/descent	640m
Difficulty	2 (route probably snowbound from November to Easter)
Walking time	6hr
High/low points	1927m/1485m
Map	Gran Sasso d'Italia (Edizioni il Lupo) (1:25,000)
Access	See Appendix B for the various ways to reach the junction
Parking	Junction at the wooden butcher's shop to the east of the road

When climbing up to Castel del Monte, beyond Ofena, on the southern approach to the high plain of Campo Imperatore, the eye is constantly drawn to the striking pyramid on the skyline that is Monte Bolza. It looks like a great peak to stand on and take in the world – but it seems too steep and rocky, with no obvious access. However…

This route is a marvellous combination of high and low – on one hand it takes in the perfect airy ridge connecting the two peaks of Monte Bolza, and on the other it offers an enclosed exploration of the great meltwater canyon on the plain. The ridge affords commanding views across the Campo and mountains that hem it, and of the distant Maiella and Abruzzo National Park peaks. Contrastingly, the wide gravelly floor and steep cliffs of the canyon evoke a remote and cut-off desert world. Being under 2000m, this route often has the advantage of being accessible when other routes are impractical – a mountain ridge for days when you want things a little easier!

Head south west towards the ridge, which forms the sky-line, passing a butcher's shop and keeping the road on the right. Follow 4x4 tracks into a depression with a large watering trough. Climb up behind and walk to the arresting white **statue**. ▸ From the statue walk west across grassland for about 1km to intersect the tarmacked road at the **riverbed**.

This is a memorial to a shepherd, with his children and dog, lost in a blizzard on the Campo many years ago as he struggled to reach the shelter of his cottage and the arms of his wife.

Cross the dry riverbed to join a 4x4 track on the other side. Follow it along the hillside parallel to the road (about 50 metres to the right). The track drops into occasional side valleys but then draws away leftwards, climbing steadily towards the bottom of the steep slope that drops from the ridge and Cima di Monte Bolza. When you are directly beneath its line, turn left and begin to climb.

The ascent is steep and unremitting, but unthreatening. A poorly defined path can be followed in places. Some 400m higher the angle eases and the ground becomes rockier. Soon you are on the **Cima di Monte Bolza** – the day's high point at just under 2000m and a wonderful crow's nest from which to survey almost the entire Campo and highest mountains of the Apennines.

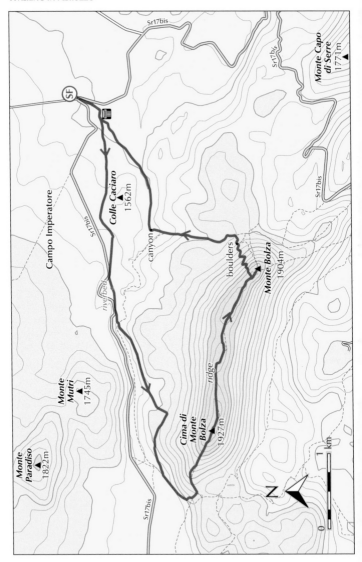

The **views** are spectacular. To the north east lie the adjacent peaks of Monte Prena and Monte Camicia. To the north, unmistakable Corno Grande stands magnificently at the end of the Campo. To the south west the ruined castle of Rocca Calascio sits on a rocky crest, with the great north east wall of Monte Sirente beyond.

Below Monte Bolza

To the south east the rounded grassy ridge runs almost level to Monte Bolza at the far end. Set off along it, kinking left at the first sub-peak to keep on the ridge proper.

On approaching **Monte Bolza**, the ridge narrows and a few pinnacles stand in the way. Turn them on the left, and then the right, if you can't go easily over. The small summit block is approached slightly to the right and up a little gully. There is a big boulder to finish and a memorial plaque just beyond.

The splendid **view** south is fully revealed. The roofs of Castel del Monte seem close by, with the broad Capestrano valley beyond and much lower. In the far distance lie the peaks of the Maiella massif, the Sulmona valley and the ranges of south Abruzzo. To the south east, the Adriatic can be glimpsed beyond

Castel del Monte from Monte Bolza

the far corner of the Campo. At the foot of the mountain is an amazing landscape of grassy pools lying among grey stony hummocks.

Go back a little to the biggest gendarme and turn right. Descend the steep north east slopes of the mountain directly and carefully, without a path, aiming for the nearest large boulders at the bottom. It might be a little easier to the right, next to a rock wall, but nothing is too daunting if taken slowly. Reach the **boulders** and easier ground and continue in the same direction towards the canyon.

You may be barked at by creamy Abruzzo sheep dogs. Ignore them and keep as far away as is reasonable and they will be happy.

Find a distinct path and possible paint splashes in a side valley leading north east to the **canyon**. Turn right and walk along the gravelly bottom of the valley, following it downstream. Occasional paint splashes might be noticed, but just stay in the riverbed. Pass by cliffs, buttresses and side valleys. Shepherds use the canyon and its side valleys as shelter for their shacks and pens. ◀

At the point where the valley opens out, leave it by a rising 4x4 track on the left. Pass over grassy mounds and pasture to the big water trough, the **statue** and back to the start point.

WALK 18

Pietracamela and Prati di Tivo

Start/finish	Mountain village of Pietracamela (42.522793, 13.553380)
Distance	7.5km
Total ascent/descent	455m
Difficulty	1 (route snowbound in winter)
Walking time	4hr
High/low points	1436m/1035m
Map	Gran Sasso d'Italia (Edizioni il Lupo) (1:25,000)
Access	Pietracamela can be reached via the SS80 road that cuts east–west across the Apennine backbone, linking Teramo and L'Aquila. A turn-off to the south lies about 7km west of the small town of Montorio al Vomano. Whether approaching from the east or west, keep a close lookout for the unassuming junction, which creeps up quickly. Follow the road for nine twisting kilometres to Pietracamela.
Parking	On the street as you drive in, just before the historic village centre

The village of Pietracamela is hidden away in a steep, forested valley north of Abruzzo's crowning peaks, Corno Grande and Corno Piccolo. From its medieval centre a path leads to the small ski resort of Prati di Tivo, returning through the wooded valley of the River Arno. Gazing on the imposing north face of Corno Piccolo from a sunny restaurant terrace in Prato di Tivo will prove irresistible. This half-day loop gives a real taste of the high Apennines without straying too far from human comforts. The route is ideally suited for the summer months, when the altitude offers a welcome respite from baking heat, but would also offer a memorable outing to the suitably equipped on a sparkling winter day.

Pietracamela is arguably the rock-climbing centre of the Apennines, with easy access to big and

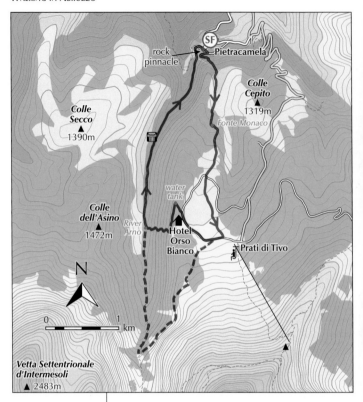

challenging routes on the north east face of Corno Piccolo. The pioneering climbing club, the Aquilotti del Gran Sasso, was formed here. Across the valley to the north west and 300m below lies the village of Intermesoli, perched in equal separation in this great forest.

From Piazza degli Ero at the entrance to the old village, climb a path, signposted to Prati di Tivo, through a little garden to the left. At a concrete road turn right and ascend to the **rock pinnacle** overlooking the village. A few metres further on, just before descending, the way goes left up a lane between restored cottages. Follow the lane up below an overhanging cliff until it reaches the top of a covered water conduit from where the path to Prati di Tivo is signposted on the right. Walk up the rising path between cliffs on the right and a stream on the left.

Emerge onto grassy meadows with patches of woodland and scrub. The first impressive sight of towering Corno Piccolo will draw you onwards, climbing gently for 1km to reach the **Fonte Monaco** in the woods. Here, two routes both lead to Prati di Tivo. Take the left-hand one, which is signposted 'Sentiero delle Traglie'. The paths run close to each other until yours climbs leftwards out of the small valley. Follow the old mule track for a further 1km until reaching the road that loops around **Prati di Tivo**.

Funghi in the Prati di Tivo woods

123

Pietracamela

Taking the lift to the top of the ridge allows for mighty views down to the Adriatic and of the north face of Corno Grande.

Cross the road and head across the meadow, passing the hotel football pitch on the left. Continue in the same direction, via an old beech tree avenue, until reaching the road again, with the main resort ski lifts opposite. ◄ There is a choice of places on the left for refreshments. Corno Piccolo and, to the right, Pizzo d'Intermesoli look impressive.

Follow the road away from the car park westwards. In 400 metres it bends right (north west) at the first hotel on the left. (Just before this, a barriered track leads obliquely across the meadow on the left. Following this track extends the walk by an hour. It leads to the Arno valley, but 2km further in. If you take it, turn right (north) when you reach the valley bottom to rejoin the description below.) Continue on the road to the **Hotel Orso Bianco** on the left. Immediately beyond, a second sealed drive slants up leftwards.

Take care as damp leaves on rocks are slippery!

Go up the drive to a large uncovered **water tank**. To the left, take a faintly waymarked path that immediately turns left (southwards) alongside a covered water course. Crags develop on the left and the path drops temporarily to round a small buttress. The path drops again to the right to begin the steep descent into the valley to the **River Arno** 200m below. ◄

At the junction with the mule track in the valley, turn right and stroll the delightful 3km back to the village along the right bank of the river. About halfway along, notice the **monument** to tragic Paolo Cichetti who succumbed here in February 1929 after being caught in a blizzard in the upper Val Maone. Wander through **Pietracamela**'s old alleyways to return to Piazza degli Ero.

WALK 19

Monte Corvo and the Val Chiarino

Start/finish	Roadside car park next to Lago di Provvidenza – on the left just before the dam when approaching from L'Aquila (42.509450, 13.407806)
Distance	23.5km
Total ascent/descent	1810m
Difficulty	3 (route probably snowbound from November to May)
Walking time	8hr
High/low points	2623m/1055m
Map	Gran Sasso d'Italia (Edizioni il Lupo) (1:25,000)
Access	Lago di Provvidenza lies alongside the SS80 road that crosses the main Gran Sasso massif between L'Aquila in the west and Teramo in the east. It's about 8km north east of Passo delle Capanelle, the highest point on the crossing. To gain the SS80 from L'Aquila, follow signs for Teramo (but not by the motorway). Similarly from Teramo, follow signs for Valle del Vomano and L'Aquila (but not by the motorway).
Parking	Lago di Provvidenza car park

A beautiful, empty valley and a big climb to a high outlying peak of the Gran Sasso group. The route is long, but easy going along the gently rising forest road. The east ridge of Monte Corvo gives a satisfying ascent through rocky ramparts. This is a lonely and wild place, where the only people you are likely to meet are shepherds, and it offers a quite different perspective on the massif away from the two 'Cornos'. The climb is high, but the reward is worth it – a wonderful day out in some of the finest scenery in Abruzzo. And if you don't want to go to the summit, the route is equally enjoyable as a shorter day walking up the lovely Piano del Castrato as far as Stazzo di Solagne.

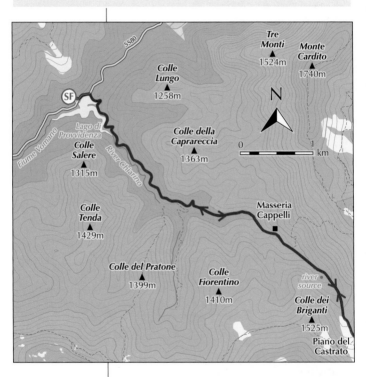

map continues on
page 128

Lago di Provvidenza is a small reservoir in the upper Vomano valley, created as part of a hydro-electric scheme. The dam allows access to the side valley of Val Chiarino – the longest in the Gran Sasso – which runs 9km south east from the Lago, defining in its upper reach the south west flank of

Monte Corvo. A forest road runs almost the whole length.

Cross the road to the lake, noticing Val Chiarino leading into the mountains opposite. Walk along the road leftwards to the dam. Cross the dam and follow the forest road around to the right. Follow the south east reach of the reservoir, which becomes the **River Chiarino**. A small suspension bridge is passed on the right. Settle into your stride and easily walk the 3km to the ruins of a fortified farm and lovely restored chapel at **Masseria Cappelli**, always staying on the main track, which may be in poor condition in parts.

From the chapel, follow the road as it ascends more steeply through thinning woods. In a few hundred metres pass, on the right, the main **river source**, which surges from underground to fill the valley bed. Carry on, past the original road head and a picnic area, to emerge magnificently from the trees onto the lush pasture of **Piano del Castrato** (a *castrato* being a bullock).

Walk through the beautiful valley to the well-kept **shepherds' rifugio**. The valley stands enticingly ahead, with Monte Corvo on the left (north east) side. Continue

Piano del Castrato

along the rough road, which starts to climb (you can cut corners along sheep paths). About 1.5km further on a second hut stands in the flat arena of **Stazzo di Solagne**.

A small canyon lies left of the building. Cross over it onto the left (true right) bank. Follow a well-trod sheep trail that climbs the side of the gorge (no waymarkings). The trail runs above the gorge, climbing to a further level area with a stone-walled **sheep pen**.

Attempting to remain on the intermittent path, follow the valley on the left as it rises steeply towards the saddle, Sella di Monte Corvo, to the right (south) of the east

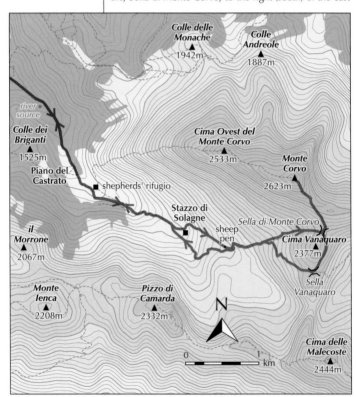

ridge of Monte Corvo – the prominent left skyline. The round, perfectly formed grassy mount to the right of the valley is Cima Vanaquaro – point 2377m on the map. It separates Sella di Monte Corvo from Sella Vanaquaro. As you suspected as you struggled up, **Sella di Monte Corvo** is a keystone to the area. ▶

At the saddle, with its obvious rock table, turn left (north) up grassy slopes towards the east ridge. There is no path, so look for paint marks on distant boulders. The route leads to a low point on the ridge to the left. Head left (north west) below the small scree slope towards a distinct slabby band below cliffs. Walk below the small slabs and follow paint marks up and across scree to the low point on the ridge.

Once on the ridge, turn left and head on up, staying on the left side and following reasonable waymarks. The rocky ramparts are impressive, but they yield easily enough as the path threads through clefts and along and back on ledges. ▶ The 2623m summit of **Monte Corvo** soon appears, with a level stroll to the cross. The views in every direction are magnificent!

East ridge of Monte Corvo

The views across the head of the remote and wild Val Vanaquaro to Pizzo d'Intermesoli and, beyond, to Corno Grande are fantastic.

At one point it's useful to use your hands briefly, but this couldn't be called a scramble.

When you are giddy with the splendour of it all, reverse the ridge back to the saddle. At this point you could turn right and descend directly to Stazzo di Solagne. However, at the cost of a little extra time and no further ascent it's more interesting to contour around the east side of Cima Venaquaro and descend to **Sella Venaquaro** on its far side. The path is poor but the way obvious. Don't lose height until you can aim for the small (possibly dry) watering hole on the Sella. From here a sheep trail wanders around the west side of the Cima, descending towards the ascent valley and the sheep pen.

Here another small diversion is worthwhile. Pass to the left of the pen rather than reversing the trail above the canyon. Follow faint paint marks and a vague path, descending but trending left, which runs behind the steep ground above Stazzo di Solagne. When the flat basin is in view, cut the easiest line rightwards and down into it.

The nearest bar is not far away – at Ortolano, 2km down the SS80 towards Teramo.

From whichever way you arrived back at the **Stazzo**, reverse the route taken earlier in the day to arrive, tired but happy, at the **Lago di Provvidenza** car park. ◀

MONTI DELLA LAGA

The path junction at Fosso della Lagnetta (Walk 21)

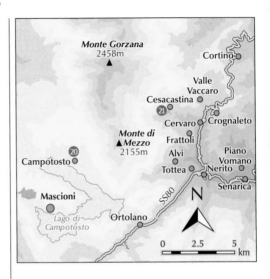

WALK 20

Monte di Mezzo circuit from Campotosto

Start/finish	Main piazza in the centre of Campotosto (42.557613, 13.369565)
Distance	16.5km
Total ascent/descent	995m
Difficulty	3 (route probably snowbound from November to Easter)
Walking time	7hr
High/low points	2155m/1337m
Map	Monti della Laga (1:25,000)
Access	The village of Campotosto is almost on the north east shore of the Lago di Campotosto, and access is easiest from the south. Take one of two roads leading north from the SS80 – the main route between Teramo to the east and L'Aquila to the west. (For further details see Appendix B.)
Parking	On the roadside near the piazza

The first of two walks in the Monti della Laga – the most northerly area in this guide and quite different from the others. Rounded, turfy sandstone peaks and characteristic rock bands reflect a changed geology. A rocky step on the lovely ascent ridge requires the use of hands in a couple of straightforward but exposed places. The views from the summit over the lake and the hills of Monti della Laga and into the heart of the Corno Grande group are fantastic. Return along the Sentiero Italia on a fine mule track, but it requires care to find it across unmarked, pathless grassy slopes and woods. Don't do the walk without the recommended map and a compass (supplemented, if possible, with a GPS that contains the route). If visibility from the ridge looks poor, leave it for another day.

From the piazza in **Campotosto**, walk north and then east along the road coming from the SS80. Descend to a bend where a **bridge** crosses the Fucino river. A large new house stands on the left. Take the track right of the house and follow the Fucino upstream (north) for a short while before crossing to its true left bank. Follow the well-defined 4x4 track north east across gently rising sheep pastures.

At a fork, keep right and head towards the entrance to a thickly wooded valley that drops from the steep west face of Monte di Mezzo, the highest point on the prominent ridge to the right (east). The track begins to rise and then swings eastwards into the valley. You may encounter grazing flocks guarded by creamy sheepdogs. ▶

Walk up the valley with the stream on the left. The way becomes a wonderful old mule track that picks a gentle route through fine beech forest. A couple of side tracks drop to the water. Don't take them – keep on. The path begins to zig-zag up through the trees and brings you onto the grassy slopes of the **Prato Andolino** which run up to the steep western face of the mountain.

Continue ahead on a good track until it reaches the streambed hard under the west face. The track swings left (north) to cross the stream. It then climbs for 1km obliquely across the west face, always headed north, until finally gaining the wide, grassy saddle of **Sella Laga**.

Avoid the dogs if you can, but if not, walk quietly and unthreateningly. They will probably bark but otherwise ignore you.

Turn right (south) at the saddle and begin the climb along the ridge. The path is indistinct but the way obvious. Stay on the ridge. Initially the climb is up steep grass, but on reaching the first high point it becomes gentler – an airy amble with inspiring views in every direction.

Beyond the second high point, a **rocky band** seems to bar progress to the summit. Don't worry: it can be passed easily enough – but it has to be done directly with hands. At the foot of the band, it is easier to move right onto the west face a little before stepping up and then moving back to the crest. On the crest, scramble up a few blocks and it is soon over. Wander on and ascend a final slope before reaching the **Monte di Mezzo** summit cairn (2155m) to the right, overlooking the village.

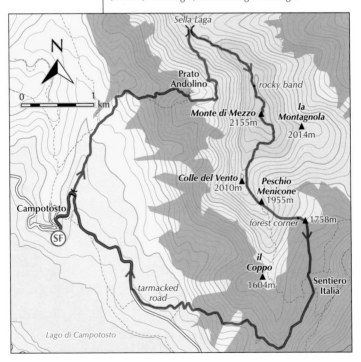

The **summit viewpoint** is exceptional. To the west the giant reservoir, Lago di Campotosto, fills the middle ground, with the village of Campotosto tucked towards the end of one of its main arms. To the east, hummocky fellside rolls up from thick forest and remote valleys (see Walk 21). And to the south east sits the magnificent Corno Grande massif – Corno Piccolo to the left, the high point of Grande in the middle, and Monte Corvo to the right.

Looking back on Prato Andolino from Sella Laga

Head south down the ridge from the summit. Stay on it for about 1.5km, over a couple of intermediate tops, until it swings more south east and you reach **Peschio Menicone**, 1955m. Below and slightly ahead, to the east (left) of the ridge, locate the first and nearest **forest corner**. Descend the steep hummocky slope east south east directly to this corner of the trees. There is neither path nor waymarks. At the corner, fork left and descend for about 150 metres along the northern edge of the wood to reach point **1758m** on the map. ▸

On the 2006 edition, red route 301 exactly marks the way to take. Unfortunately it is not signed on the ground.

Turn right and enter the woods. There is no obvious path. Head south and descend through the trees, possibly quite steeply and slightly to the left, to emerge after 200 metres in a small clearing. Cross the clearing southwards and re-enter the trees. A track is now more evident. Continue on the same line through the brief tree band to enter a long meadow enclosed by forest. Walk directly ahead, southwards, across the meadow. After about 300 metres, trees protrude slightly from the left. Behind them find, with some relief, the obvious and signed **Sentiero Italia**.

Turn right (south west) along the Sentiero Italia (marked '300' to Campotosto) and return to the forest. The path is now a wonderful old mule track. Follow it as it gently descends towards the village. It swings right (north west), and views across the lake open out. Always follow red markings where side tracks join, keeping to the main route. The trees thin as height is lost. The last section crosses meadows to join a **tarmacked road** that emerges on the main lakeside road about 2km south of the village.

Turn left and walk along the road back to the piazza in **Campotosto**. Signposts and the map suggest the Sentiero Italia takes a track to the village on the other side of the road, but this way has been blocked in recent years. It is easier to follow the quiet road.

Summit of Monte di Mezzo

WALK 21

Cima della Laghetta and Monte Gorzano

Start/finish	Near the war memorial in the centre of Cesacastina (42.588802, 13.448026)
Distance	18km
Total ascent/descent	1510m
Difficulty	3; or 2 if omitting the ridge and peaks. (Route probably snowbound from November to Easter.)
Walking time	7hr 30min
High/low points	2458m/1143m
Map	Monti della Laga (1:25,000)
Access	The village of Cesacastina lies north of the Val Vormano, from where it is best approached via the SS80 – the main Apennine route between Teramo to the east and L'Aquila to the west. Coming from Teramo, turn off right (northwards) onto the SP45A, near the village of Negrito, and follow the twisting road north up the Zingano valley for 6km or so to a turn-off for Cesacastina. Signs for Cesacastina (and Cervaro and Frattoli) should be evident. The road is OK but not in the best of conditions, so take care. It winds up to the small village about 6km away.
Parking	On the road, Piazza San Pietro, near the memorial and play park

A second exploration of the Monti della Laga and the most northerly route in this book. This is a big mountain walk of great variety and charm, with lofty exposure along a very fine mountain ridge (although a significant shortcut is available). Access is from the remote village of Cesacastina on the eastern side of the mountain, making this route particularly suitable for those based in the Teramo area.

Monte Gorzano, at 2458m, is the high point of the walk – and indeed the high point of the massif. It is a perfect spot to linger. The ascent requires a determined, but not excessive, effort; the journey along the ridge, traversing Cima della Laghetta, seems to float by and is substantial reward for the haul up the grassy slopes. The return through the woods is delightful, with the river often cascading over bands of rock.

Halfway up, a path can be followed directly to the Stazzo Cento Fonti and the descent route, which allows the ridge and peaks to be omitted completely while still giving a wonderful walk over a shorter day. On the other hand, the southern part of the route runs very close to Sella Laga, which features on Walk 20. A linking of the two may be possible for those seeking further adventure.

Starting at the church near the play park and war memorial in **Cesacastina**, walk south west, left of the brown sign indicating the way to Fosso dell'Acero, along Via Borgo (which becomes Via Fontana Vechia). This is the route of the Sentiero Italia (S.I.) – path 300/300I. Continue beyond the last house to a signpost at a track junction by a small **chapel**, passing a delightful old fountain and water trough on the right. Take the rising track to the right, signed 'S.I. 300I', for Campotosto.

The track climbs the hillside, via gentle zig-zags, to reach another signpost and a 4x4 road. Go left along the level road and soon swing left over the river to reach a track junction at a chain between green metal posts. Turn

Old fountain and water trough

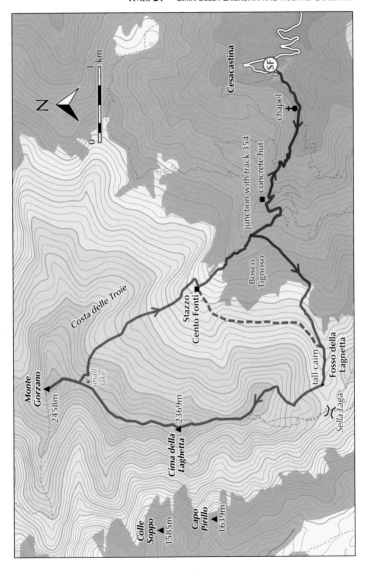

The tall cairn just before Sella Laga

right to pass between the posts and up the rising track to a block-built **concrete hut** belonging to 'ENEL'.

Take the path that climbs from the right of the hut and goes behind it. Follow it through trees, a little steeply in places, to emerge onto grass at a bend of a 4x4 track that comes up from the left. From the bend, turn right up a path and back into the forest to join, straightaway, another 4x4 track. Walk right along the track, which swings left and rises parallel to the river below.

At the **junction with track 354** that arrives on the right, go left and continue on up (path S.I. 300I). The track climbs in the forest before emerging onto grassland. The route now goes obliquely right to climb the grassy slopes. Take care to spot a red-and-white waymark on a tree ahead and up on the right. (Do not follow the level path across the grass and back into the trees.)

Climb, following occasional waymarks, to reach a bigger path that contours the hillside. The emerging view, southwards to the Corno Grande peaks, is magnificent. The route turns left along the bigger path and climbs, more gently, towards the head of the valley that drops from Sella Laga. ◄

Beautiful Monte di Mezzo lies ahead, visited on Walk 20.

At **Fosso della Lagnetta** the path reaches the valley bed. A signpost points a way sharp right to Stazzo Cento Fonti (path 305 (TO)). This is the shortcut that misses out the ridge and peaks – if you want to take it, reducing your day by roughly half, go right and contour the hillside down to the Stazzo to resume the route description from there. But for the full route, continue on up to reach a **tall cairn** just before the pass.

At the cairn, go half-right (north west) and climb to the skyline, first on a shaly rib and then, in the same line, to the right of a shallow gully. ▶ Turn right at a cairn and follow metal posts steeply up the hillside to the ridge ahead and on the right. At the skyline, turn left to climb further up the ridge, still following posts, to the first top and the beginning of the crest (which is now the border of Abruzzo and Lazio).

The huge view to the west, over Lago di Campotosto, is revealed for the first time.

A waterfall among the Cento Fonti

141

The panorama is inspirational; the view down the ribbed crests that rise from the westerly forests is giddying. Enjoy the moment!

The ridge dips, rises and rolls onwards to reach **Cima della Laghetta**, at 2369m, in about 1km. Traverse the peak and continue for a further 1km until above the **small lake** on the right. The path continues along the ridge, which rises steeply one final time and then eases to lead to the summit cairn of **Monte Gorzano** (2458m), some 200 metres ahead. ◄

Retrace your steps towards the little lake. Just before it, turn from the ridge and go leftwards, over level ground, to a prominent waymark post on a lesser ridge. The post, which marks the start of the descent route, is a fine viewpoint, with the Corno Grande massif to the south and the wide, wild eastern amphitheatre of Monte Gorzano at your feet.

Head down (south east) across rough grassland, aiming for the forest at the base of the prominent ridge, the **Costa delle Troie**, to the left. There is no path. Follow posts and cairns the whole way. Each successive marker should be visible from the one you are at – look carefully for them. In places, though, they are sparse. If you lose the markers, don't worry – aim for the trees just right of the stream valley. The line is pretty direct and always right of the stream below Costa delle Troie. ◄ A path finally develops before you reach a 4x4 track, a signpost and a bridge over the stream.

The waypoints on a GPS device would be useful here but not essential.

At the signpost, go right towards **Stazzo Cento Fonti**, the green metal hut nearby. Just before the Stazzo, turn left at a signpost onto path 354, which leads down grassy slopes on the right bank of the small river and into the forest – the Bosco Tignoso. (This signpost is where the shortcut along path 305 returns to.) The path passes a notable waterfall, one of many, and a picnic area before soon rejoining the ascent route (path 300I) to complete the circuit. Reverse the ascent route all the way back to **Cesacastina**.

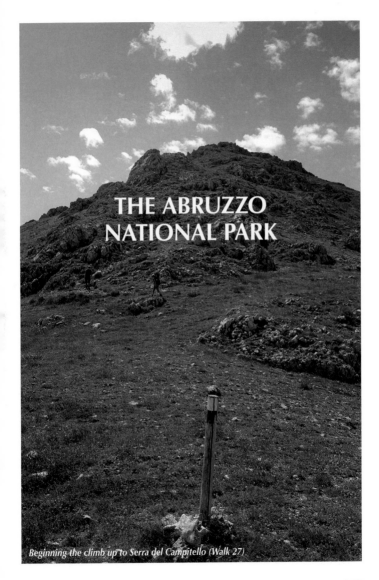

THE ABRUZZO NATIONAL PARK

Beginning the climb up to Serra del Campitello (Walk 27)

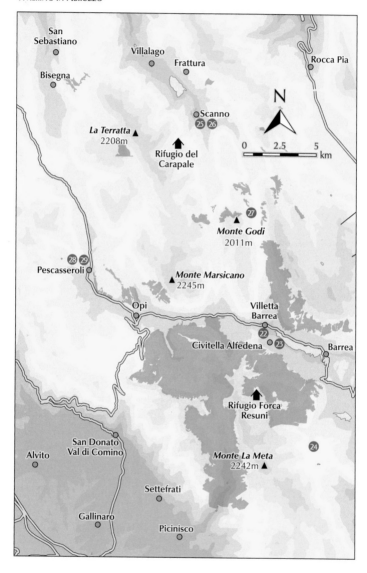

WALK 22
Villetta Barrea and Civitella Alfedena

Start/finish	Villetta Barrea – small car park by the bridge over the Sangro (41.774988, 13.934294)
Distance	8km
Total ascent/descent	345m
Difficulty	1 (route snowbound for some of the winter)
Walking time	4hr
High/low points	1212m/967m
Map	Monti Marsicani (1:25,000)
Access	The village of Villetta Barrea lies along the Upper Sangro river in the centre of the Abruzzo National Park. Drivers will probably approach from the town of Castel di Sangro to the south east, but it can also be reached from Pescasseroli and Scanno. (For further details see Appendix B.) Villetta is linked to Castel di Sangro and Pescasseroli by a regular bus service.
Parking	Car park on the right over the bridge in Villetta Barrea. Starting in Civitella is an alternative – use the upper car park at the equestrian centre.

A short but wonderfully varied exploration of the heart of the Abruzzo National Park. The circuit links two of the most attractive and beautifully preserved villages in the park, taking in a fine wood of black pine and beech, open limestone meadow, an ancient sheep drove and a return stretch along the banks of the Barrea lake. The views of the Upper Sangro valley are tremendous, and there is even a chance to spot a wolf! (Should the charms of Civitella Alfedena detain you longer than planned, you can return quickly to Villetta by walking down the road that links the two villages.)

Head up the path immediately left of the car park in **Villetta Barrea**, signed 'H3', into the black pine forest. The way runs west above the Sangro and Villetta Barrea opposite, and climbs peacefully and gently for about 1km

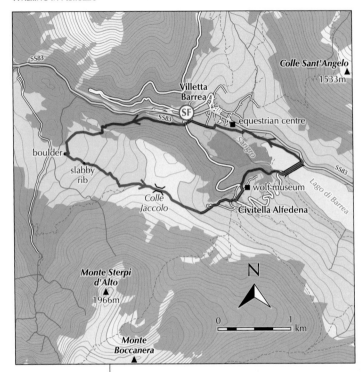

before swinging left and rising more steeply, with a few zig-zags, to exit the forest at the crest of the hill.

A wonderful **view** opens out. The forested, craggy amphitheatre of the Camosciara dominates in the distance, with a patchwork of soft lawns and scrub lying between.

The path heads slightly to the right and descends across turf, through thickets and over broken-down stone walls towards the road through the valley. Contour around a shallow gully to reach a large **boulder** on the right with directions painted on it. Turn left to face a small **slabby rib** with paint marks. This is path G3. Climb it south east over scrub towards a saddle, Colle Jaccolo, 1km away.

> The way is the **ancient sheep drove**, or *tratturo*, linking Pescasseroli with Candela, 140km to the south east in Puglia. It's not unusual to encounter a shepherd and flock watched over by half a dozen Abruzzo sheep dogs.

Reach a welcome fountain on **Colle Jaccolo** – the high point of the walk. The view back up the Sangro valley is magnificent. The route continues straight and obvious in the same direction, now as a white track, for a further 1km to the tarmac, turning steeply left down into **Civitella Alfedena**. ▶

On the left is the alternative car park for those choosing to start the walk in Civitella.

Follow the cobbled lane down through the well-preserved old houses, passing the new community centre then turning right after a few hundred metres to join the tarmac road outside a café. Turn left and go downhill to reach another café and the **wolf museum**, with wolf compound behind (it's worth a small diversion to look over the wall and see if you can see the small, shy family group that live there – a lane leads from the right side of the museum).

Civitella Alfedena

Turn left at the museum. You may decide to continue down the road to Villetta, but the full route, path I3, soon turns right at the last building, following a lane behind and to the left of the church on the knoll. Continue down through woodland before reaching the bridge that links Civitella with the main road along the **Barrea lake** (a manmade reservoir that fits harmoniously into this wonderful landscape).

Cross the bridge and turn left along the road, then at the earliest opportunity take a path along the water's edge. Continue along the lake north westwards towards Villetta. At the large **equestrian centre** near the village, head left back towards the River Sangro and follow the path along its bank into the centre of **Villetta Barrea**. Cross the river by a wooden footbridge, pass the hydro-electricity museum, and go up to the car park.

WALK 23

The Val di Rose

Start/finish	Upper car park in Civitella Alfedena, just before the riding centre (41.764842, 13.938396)
Distance	12.5km
Total ascent/descent	985m
Difficulty	3 (route probably snowbound from November to April)
Walking time	6hr
High/low points	1975m/1104m
Map	Monti Marsicani (1:25,000)
Access	Civitella Alfedena is in the centre of the Abruzzo National Park, in the forest above the north western end of Lago di Barrea. From the SS17 at Castel di Sangro take the SS83 towards Barrea and then on to Civitella at the far end of the lake. Reach Civitella across the lake bridge or from Villetta Barrea. (For further details see Appendix B.)
Parking	Car park at the top of Civitella Alfedena

This is probably the most acclaimed walk in the Abruzzo National Park, from above the beautiful village of Civitella Alfedena to the highest of its mountain ridges. The magnificent circuit combines meadow, beech forest, high alpine pasture, steep crags, a lonely mountain hut and an exposed ridge – with a good chance of encountering chamois on the crags above the tree line. The ground at the head of the valley is particularly beautiful, with fantastic views down into the Upper Sangro valley. The return is via the long and secluded Val Jannanghera, which emerges midway above the Lago di Barrea.

The route is closed in July and August to protect the young chamois. Autumn is particularly recommended, when the eerie booming of rutting red deer stags and cracking of locked antlers adds to the splendid landscape. And the very scarce Marsican bear is known to frequent the lonely depths of Val Jannanghera – don't forget your binoculars!

The previously published description of this route included an optional ascent of Monte Petroso – the high point of the Abruzzo National Park – from Rifugio di Forca Resuni. It has now been omitted as the national park wishes to protect the summit by limiting visitor traffic.

From the upper car park, walk down the cobbled street to the centre of **Civitella Alfedena**, passing the town hall on the right. About 50 metres before the street turns right to the tarmacked road, the Val di Rose is signposted along a side street on the right (indicated as route I/1). A few metres down the side street, the Val Di Rose is signposted again to the right. Turn right and climb out of the village, crossing the new road to the car park, and then go up stone steps to a lane through stone-walled meadows. The beech forest is soon reached.

The **Val di Rose** becomes apparent as the path steepens to enter it. At first the way is through woods and over grassy shoulders, but soon the splendid forest encroaches and deepens. The beech trees are huge and magnificent. The isolation builds as you climb gently. The way is always obvious and the path good. ▸

Occasional clearings allow fine views to the rocky valley head and back to Lago di Barrea.

About 3km from the village the path enters the wonderful upper valley. You are in the chamois (*camosci*) zone and, if quiet, may be treated to a close-up view of

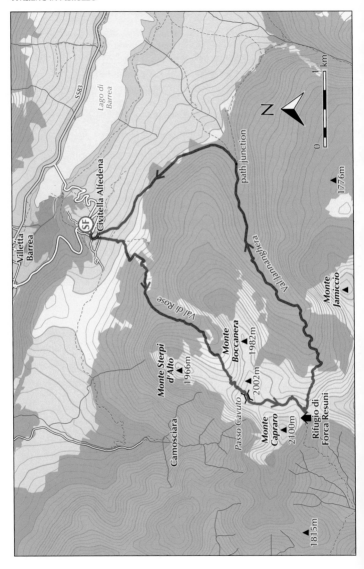

Autumn beeches in the Val di Rose

the large family group that lives on these ramparts. The path leads up through the end of the valley to the alpine pasture of **Passo Cavuto**.

> The **panorama** is magnificent – south towards the rocky summit of Monte Petroso and north west into the plunging forests, towers and cliffs of the Camosciara valley. It's a magical place.

151

Cut a level way across the pasture and onto the shoulder beyond, trending always southwards towards the amphitheatre at the head of the Val Jannanghera. In the autumn you may be lucky enough to watch red deer stags locking antlers in the battle for mating rights with the hinds who graze nonchalantly around. Beyond a promontory the **Rifugio di Forca Resuni** stands starkly silhouetted on the saddle. Walk to the hut.

> The **rifugio** is a very fine place for lunch on a dry and calm day, with the views south and west into the forests of Lazio particularly fine. It is usually locked but a basic winter room is always open, should rudimentary shelter be needed.

Take the path down from the hut to the east and into the amphitheatre at the head of the **Val Jannanghera**. The tree line is reached and silent forest re-entered. The path, signed 'K6' in places, remains largely obvious for the long descent. At times alternatives present themselves, but keep mainly to the valley floor and you won't go wrong. The darkness and solitude are atmospheric, with brief welcome open meadows. Eventually, after 3.5km, an obvious **path junction** is reached.

Rifugio di Forca Resuni

Take the left-hand track, which may be signed 'I/4'. This turns north and then north westwards towards Civitella. It skirts the entrance to the Val Jannanghera, keeping the forest to the left and fields down to the lake on the right. The path finally runs through stone-walled fields to houses on the edge of **Civitella Alfedena**. Follow the lane and then cobbled street to the welcoming cafés of the village centre.

WALK 24
Monte La Meta and the Mainarde crest

Start/finish	Car park at the rifugio on Pianora Campitelli, west of Alfedena (41.700467, 13.981751)
Distance	17.5km
Total ascent/descent	1160m
Difficulty	3; or 2 if omitting Monte La Meta and the crest. (Route very likely to be snowbound from November to May.)
Walking time	7hr
High/low points	2242m/1408m
Map	Monti Marsicani – Mainarde (1:25,000)
Access	Pianora Campitelli is accessed by a good mountain road up from the village of Alfedena, just outside the Abruzzo National Park in the far south of Abruzzo. (For further details see Appendix B.)
Parking	Car park at the rifugio

A visit to a great mountain crossroads at the southern tip of Abruzzo and, optionally, the beautiful peak above. This is a journey into a pristine mountain environment, following tracks established over millennia by the ancients who herded, traded and lived here. The route traces a line into, out of and along the borders of three regions – Abruzzo, Lazio and Molise – passing through thick native forest and across spectacular mountainside. It's a marginal call for a collection of walks in Abruzzo, but its inclusion is easily justified.

The route serves as a hub, allowing variations to the main walk described, and easier days as a result. The ascent of Monte La Meta can be left out, as can the exploration of the Mainarde crest to the south east, leaving just a circuit up to and down from the Passo dei Monarci – a very worthwhile outing in itself.

Before you set out, check the route, if you can, on the Abruzzo National Park website (www.parcoabruzzo.it) – paths are sometimes closed in high summer to afford added protection to the breeding wildlife.

From the car park at the rifugio in the north corner of the **Pianora Campitelli**, a track (signed occasionally 'L1') leads north west into beech woods. Walk along it and swing leftwards up and into the mature forest. The way climbs steadily, quite steeply in places, and consistently

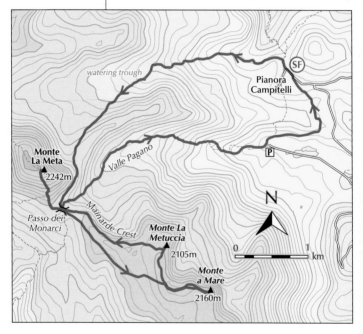

westwards through the beautiful trees to emerge after 1.8km onto the open hillside.

The path now veers south west and cuts a direct line up the turf-covered slope, passing small rocky outcrops and, on the right, the foundations of a long-gone homestead and a **watering trough**. Ahead lies the impressive rocky bulk of Monte La Meta with its sub-summit to the left. The great open slopes of the corrie sweep away to the right.

The efficient route soon reaches the broad ridge that separates the corrie from the adjacent Valle Pagano, and which is the border of Abruzzo and Molise. ▶ The path cleverly skirts the south face of Monte La Meta, with no more than minor dips and rises through boulders and across scree, to reach **Passo dei Monarci**. There are very fine views in all directions – an obvious place to refresh and choose from three options for your continued walk.

The most straightforward choice would be the descent down the Valle Pagano (see 'Once again at **Passo dei Monarci**, descend the Valle Pagano...', in the description below); or you could set off along the Mainarde crest to visit the peak of Monte a Mare and then return to the pass (see 'Alternatively, to follow the crest, walk south east from the pass on a path parallel with the crest...'); or you could climb Monte La Meta, which stands

The summit of Monte La Meta with the Mainarde crest beyond

The view is now to the south and east, across the head of Valle Pagano, to the Passo dei Monarci.

commandingly above you, and then return to the pass. The last of these options is now described.

Turn north east to face Monte La Meta and climb the path that leads from the pass obliquely rightwards and steeply up the grassy south west flank of the mountain to the rocky ridge 100 metres back and left of the summit. With some effort, reach the rocks and then swing back right to follow the ridge to the cross and metal sculpture on **Monte La Meta**'s 2242m summit.

> The **view** is exceptional, across all of the mountains of the national park and deep into Lazio to the south and west. Monte Petroso, in particular, stands proud at the north western end of the ridge.

When you can avert your gaze, carefully reverse your steps to **Passo dei Monarci**.

There are two options now: descent, or a simple walk along the Mainarde crest to climb Monte a Mare – prominent but not high – about 2km distant. To descend, see 'Once again at **Passo dei Monarci**, descend the Valle Pagano…', below. Alternatively, to follow the crest, walk south east from the pass on a path parallel with the crest but about 100 metres back from it. There are sporadic paint marks, but make your own way using the crest line

The head of Valle Pagano

as your guide. The way undulates, dropping into hollows and climbing small promitories, but overall it is level. Draw closer to the ridge on your left as you approach **Monte a Mare** and, for the final brief ascent, take the ridge itself.

> Once more the **views** are spectacular, this time particularly down into the Val Fiorita to the north east, where a watering hole (which may be dry) and road-head car park are easy to spot.

To return to the pass, retrace the way you came or, more interestingly, follow the line of the crest back (the border of Lazio and Molise). This will take longer, but not much, and traverses the intervening 2105m top of **Monte La Metuccia**.

Once again at **Passo dei Monarci**, descend the Valle Pagano, which drops north eastwards from the saddle. Follow the obvious path down the bed of the incipient valley, among rocks, and then onto grass to the left of the valley bottom. The path gently decends the beautiful valley towards the tree line and soon the forest is re-entered. Go steadily down through the silence for about 1.5km until the ground begins to level, the trees open out and you are in the **car park** at the head of Val Fiorita.

Turn left and cross the car park to reach a picnic site that runs up and into the forest. Take some care to locate a small path at the bottom right of the trees, which goes right across the open hillside. Follow the path as it climbs gently and later becomes a defined but rarely used track that continues a rising contour of the hillside above the waterhole on your right. Sporadic waymarks may be spotted.

The track reaches the ridge and swings left around it before continuing north for 100 metres to a more defined white 4x4 track. Turn left and walk along the track, keeping right at a fork, to cross grassland towards trees 150 metres away. Go through the trees to find **Pianora Campitelli** with the rifugio and car park in the far corner. Cross the pasture to the car park.

WALK 25
La Terratta

Start/finish	Ski lift station in Scanno (41.900484, 13.878197)
Distance	14km
Total ascent/descent	1295m
Difficulty	3 (route probably snowbound from November to April)
Walking time	6hr 30min
High/low points	2208m/1025m
Map	Monti Marsicani (1:25,000)
Access	The small town of Scanno lies in the south of the region just north east of the Abruzzo National Park. It can be reached from the north after passing through the narrow Sagittario gorge on the SR479 from Anversa degli Abruzzi and the Sulmona valley. It can also be reached on this same road from Villetta Barrea to the south via the Passo Godi. It's a popular spot and, despite being remote, has a regular bus service to Anversa, Sulmona and on to Rome.
Parking	Ski station car park. The road climbs from the lake into the town to arrive at the edge of the historic centre and main piazza. Opposite the piazza and immediately after the main road turns right, take the one-way side road on the right that leads to the large car park. From Villetta turn left for the car park about 200 metres before the piazza.

From the busy shores of Lago di Scanno, a forested valley leads enticingly into high mountains on the western side. The valley is narrow, silent and long – a steep and memorable ascent directly to the 2208m summit of La Terratta – a tremendous viewpoint into the Abruzzo National Park, to the wide, flat floor of the Fucino basin, to the mountains of the Sirente and back to the blue lake far below. Return along the broad, high ridge, typical of the Abruzzo Apennines, which forms part of the park border, and down the equally fine adjacent valley to ancient Scanno town centre. (Although the ridge is broad and marked, route-finding may be confusing in poor visibility. Be sure of a clear day.)

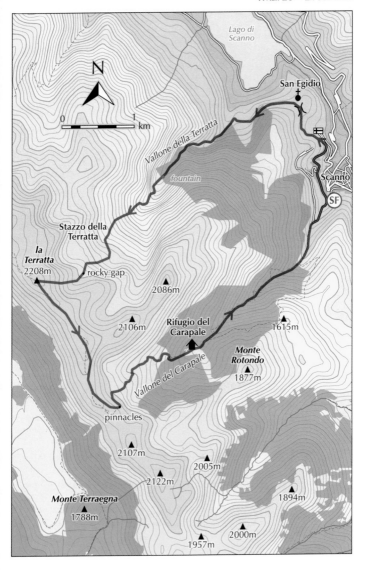

Lago di Scanno from La Terratta summit

A 10min diversion allows a visit to the little church of San Egidio, which stands up on the right.

From the car park in **Scanno**, head north along Via Domenico di Rienzo. Pass hotels and apartment blocks for about 500 metres until you swing right, and in another 200 metres meet a road ascending from the right. Turn left up the quiet lane that serves a quarry, soon passing the **cemetery** on the right. After about 600 metres the sealed lane turns left at a block-built quarry building. Take the footpath on the right and climb quickly to a **saddle** with a fountain. ◄

From the fountain, descend towards Lago di Scanno. The path levels and widens into an old mule track, which leads north west and then contours (left) to the west. A rocky viewpoint on the right offers great views across the lake to the small village of Frattura on the flanks of Monte Genzana. Follow the level track as it passes through woods and into meadows. Ahead lies the dense forest and rocky outcrops of the **Vallone della Terratta**. The path swings right to join a 4x4 track; follow it steeply down.

At the bottom, a side path with a red-and-white waymark crosses the stream and heads up the valley. Follow it. At first the way is almost level, gently rising through the narrow confines and wonderful woodland, but soon it steepens. Keep going, pausing to catch your breath and absorb the solitude. Pass a mossy old **fountain** and trough at half-height (1477m) and prepare for the final zig-zags through the trees. Soon enough you emerge into the rocky pasture of the **Stazzo della Terratta**.

Cross the meadow past boulders, creeping shrubs and increasingly lonely beech trees. The path heads slightly left to ascend a gap through a steeper section and gain the next level of the corrie. A distinct low cliff stands ahead. Now the way wanders rightwards and up through the boulder field to a **rocky gap** in the cliff on the right. Pass through and enter the big bowl of the summit slopes. Follow the depression and then go a little to the right. Leave it to begin an exhausting oblique climb up the grassy slope to **La Terratta** (2208m), which lies unseen up to the right.

> The **substantial cairn** affords magnificent views in every direction. The Lago di Scanno appears as a little patch of blue way below. Beyond it rise Monte Genzana, then Monte Rotella and, finally, to the left, Monte Amaro at the heart of the Maiella massif. To the south stands the Marsicano group in the centre of the Abruzzo National Park, with the remote plain of Terraegna lying between.

The broad ridge runs away in both directions. Turn south east and descend happily across small stones and patches of tough grass. Cairns mark the way until the Vallone del Carapale appears on the north east (left) side. Continue around the corrie rim towards distinct twin rock **pinnacles** below the ridge in the southern corner.

Locate the path on the left and descend into the amphitheatre across scree and through boulders. ▶ The path leads carefully towards the establishing valley. The infrastructure of the Scanno ski resort is obvious below and to the right. Enter the trees and go down to the old shepherds' hut, **Rifugio del Carapale**. Abandoned ski lift equipment litters the valley at one point but is quickly passed.

The sub-alpine, almost primeval atmosphere here is fantastic.

Continue easily down the old mule track and through forest without further ado until the cables of the main ski lift appear above. Walk beneath and alongside them until the sealed road is reached and soon thereafter the car park.

Scanno may seem a world away from the remote wilderness you were so recently immersed in, but the houses and churches of the historical centre are as much a part of this harmonious landscape as the mountain tops and empty forests.

WALK 26

The Scanno town and lake loop

Start/finish	Ski lift station in Scanno (41.900484, 13.878197)
Distance	8km
Total ascent/descent	375m
Difficulty	1 (route may be snowbound for some of the winter)
Walking time	3hr
High/low points	1090m/930m
Map	Monti Marsicani (1:25,000)
Access	The small town of Scanno lies in the south of the region just north east of the Abruzzo National Park. It can be reached from the north after passing through the narrow Sagittario gorge on the SR479 from Anversa degli Abruzzi and the Sulmona valley. It can also be reached on this same road from Villetta Barrea to the south via the Passo Godi. It's a popular spot and, despite being remote, has a regular bus service to Anversa, Sulmona and on to Rome.
Parking	Ski station car park. The road climbs from the lake into the town to arrive at the edge of the historic centre and main piazza. Opposite the piazza and immediately after the main road turns right, take the one-way side road on the right that leads to the large car park. From Villetta turn left for the car park about 200 metres before the piazza.

Exploring the small mountain town of Scanno, in the upper reaches of the Sagittario valley, and the nearby lake is almost an Abruzzo 'must do'. This tremendously varied half-day stroll delivers the best of both, linking the two via a lovely old mule track that offers a tantalising glimpse of the wild Terratta valley. Along the way swimming spots, viewpoints, cafés and old churches will detain all but the most determined.

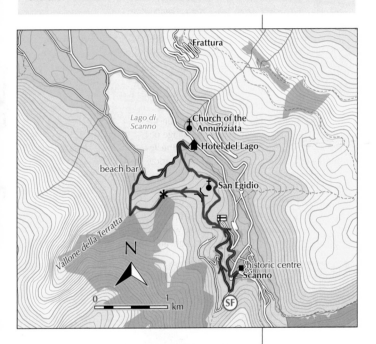

Scanno is the nearest thing that inland Abruzzo has to a tourist trap, but if you are looking for coach parks, souvenir shops and fast-food outlets you will be disappointed. Instead you will find a centuries-old village centre, beautifully preserved, in a spectacular mountain setting with a pretty lake close by. In summer it's certainly busier than most places in the region, and the number of hotels and lakeside developments are at a comfortable maximum, but the natural splendour cannot be diminished.

From the car park, head north along Via Domenico di Rienzo. Pass hotels and apartment blocks for about 500 metres until you swing right, and in another 200 metres meet a road ascending from the right. Turn left up the quiet lane that serves a quarry, soon passing the **cemetery** on the right. After about 600 metres the sealed lane turns left at a block-built quarry building. Take the footpath on the right and climb quickly to a **saddle** with a fountain. ◄

A 10min diversion allows a visit to the little church of San Egidio, which stands up on the right.

From the fountain, descend towards Lago di Scanno. The path levels and widens into a lovely old mule track, which leads north west and then contours to the west. A rocky **viewpoint** on the right gives great views across the lake to the village of Frattura on the flanks of Monte Genzana. Follow the level track as it passes through woods and into meadows. Ahead lies the dense forest and rocky outcrops of the Vallone della Terratta. The path swings right to join a 4x4 track; follow it steeply down leftwards. ◄

This is where Walk 25 departs up the valley to the summit of La Terratta.

At the bottom, turn sharp right along the track that leads to the lake with a welcome **beach bar** and swimming spot. Turn right and walk around the southern shore,

Scanno

Cooling off

passing bars, restaurants and hotels before reaching the large **Hotel del Lago** in the south east corner of the lake. (From here you can take a diversion to the **Church of the Annunziata**, built, unusually, straddling the main valley road 500 metres along the lakeside. The frescoes are wonderful.)

Behind the hotel a footpath steps up from the road and into the woods. It contours back above the lakeside road before turning left to climb through the trees. After several zig-zags the path straightens to reach an unsealed lane by a small new building.

Turn left and follow the lane as it contours around the hill (on which sits San Egidio church). Scanno soon comes into view. The lane leads towards the **cemetery**, which it passes to join the sealed quarry road that was walked earlier. Turn left and return to the junction with Via Domenico di Rienzo. You could turn right to the car park, but instead continue down the hill to reach the main road into **Scanno**.

Turn right and follow the road up, past the town hall on the left and Tamoil garage on the right, until it swings left across a bridge to reach the main piazza and traffic-free **historic centre**. Hopefully you will have time to wander through its ancient alleyways, past splendid churches and buildings. Opposite the piazza is the road that leads in a few minutes back to the car park.

WALK 27

Serra del Campitello and Monte Godi

Start/finish	Roadside car park on the SR489 600m north of Passo Godi (41.845466, 13.925763)
Distance	25km
Total ascent/descent	1290m
Difficulty	3; or 2 if omitting the Campitello ridge and Monte Godi. (Route probably snowbound from November to April.)
Walking time	7hr
High/low points	2026m/1555m
Map	Monti Marsicani (1:25,000)
Access	Passo Godi lies at the head of the broad valley that runs south into the Abruzzo National Park from Scanno. It is on the SR479 road and can be approached from Scanno in the north or from Villetta Barrea in the south. (See Appendix B for further details.)
Parking	In the car park, which is on the right when approaching from Scanno and 600 metres before (north of) the hotel and restaurants at Passo Godi itself.

A day of variety and solitude in the remote heart of the Marsican mountains, this route wanders delightfully through a secluded corner of the Abruzzo National Park, striking a perfect balance of pasture, forest, ridges and high peaks.

The route follows good 4x4 tracks across the pasture and through forest, linking old shepherds' huts and spring-fed troughs where flocks are brought to drink. The going is surprisingly gentle – with, of course, some up and down!

Above the huts, the tracks become paths which are good and mostly waymarked. At one point the path is left behind and a steep mountain slope is ascended to gain the ridge that links Serra del Campitello with Monte del Campitello. Although it can be bypassed, this crest is recommended – a great experience of Apennine ridge walking for relatively little effort. A good opportunity, too, to observe red deer at the fringes of the forest and groups of chamois on the craggy ledges.

The final ascent to Monte Godi is also optional but recommended; if you've got the energy it's a fine way to end the day – and it provides the best view of all.

▶ From the car park, walk north west along the track (shown as 'Y1' on park maps) into the open valley, with Monte Godi on your left. After 350 metres, where the track turns sharp right, cut a corner by continuing straight ahead. The way becomes rockier and steeper but soon the two tracks reunite.

Go left and easily onwards, gently desending towards the pasture (not yet in view) that lies behind Monte Godi. The ridge between Serra and Monte del Campitello is the left end of the skyline ahead, and the prominent peak to the right is Serra Capra Morta ('Dead Goat Mountain'). The track passes briefly through trees and arrives at the shepherds' rifugio of **Stazzo di Ziomas**. In the summer

Passo Godi is a major watershed of the region and home to a small ski resort as well as a couple of hotels and restaurants.

Stazzo Campo Rotondo

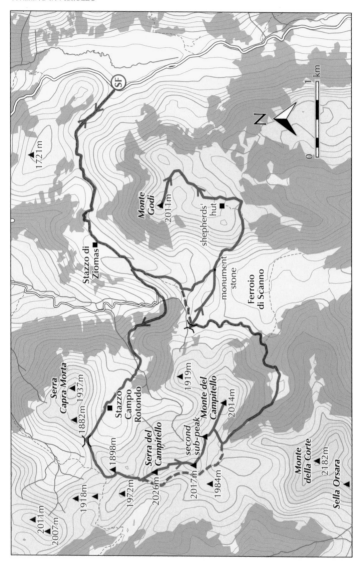

there will probably be sheep dogs here – ignore them and keep as far away as is reasonable, and they will be happy.

Pass the hut on the right and walk south westwards for 400 metres to a junction where a track goes right and then swings left to drop steeply to the head of the valley. Go right and down the track. Near the bottom, just beyond cliffs on the left, a track forks left; go left along this rising track and follow it into the forest. Keep along the delightful track, going through trees, across clearings and at one point climbing briefly but steeply, until you are in the pasture of another shepherds' hut, the **Stazzo Campo Rotondo**.

Notice a path behind the hut that climbs the hillside obliquely to reach a saddle at the bottom of the ridge that drops from the summit of Serra Capra Morta on the right. Go right of the hut and walk up the path. At the **saddle**, turn left and follow the path south west along a low ridge and then across hillside that slopes down to the right.

Reach a small saddle and go over it, following occasional red-topped marker posts, to then traverse another hillside, heading southwards on a less well-defined path to reach a third saddle. You are now at the base of the steep but relatively short north slope of **Serra del Campitello**, the summit of which is 100m above.

If you don't want to walk along the ridge and visit the summits, from the saddle you could continue along the path southwards – it descends a little and crosses open hillside, keeping the ridge alongside and above you, always on your left – to reach the forest after 1.5km, and then resume the description below from '...follow the good path through beautiful woodland and tranquil clearings'.

However, to walk the ridge, turn left at the saddle and ascend the pathless slope steeply to the summit cairn. The lovely ridge runs away to the south, then curves leftwards to the rounded grassy summit of Monte del Campitello, about 1.7km away. Walk along it, easily passing over the first sub-peak and then climbing to the **second** before passing it a little to the right. There is no

The ridge to Monte del Campitello

path, but all is obvious and you will soon enough reach the 2014m summit of **Monte del Campitello**.

> The **views** are wonderful – in particular, south-wards to the wild corrie below the summit of Monte Marsicano; south eastwards into the peaks of Monti della Meta; and north eastwards to nearby Monte Godi. You might decide now if you're going to climb Monte Godi, so take a good look at the line!

From the summit, retrace your steps back along the ridge to where you can descend, with some care, left-wards (south) down the grassy slope (probably just before the **second sub-peak**) to rejoin the path you quit at the saddle. Turn left and follow the good path through beautiful woodland and tranquil clearings, descending gently the whole way.

The route goes first south east and then swings east to arrive at a junction with a 4x4 track in the trees. Turn left to emerge soon onto the great pasture of **Ferroio di Scanno**.

Walk north along the track, passing after 500 metres a watering trough down to the right. The track rises to a low **saddle** and swings rightwards around the left end of the low crest, at which point you have two options.

If you don't want to visit the Pope's monument or climb Monte Godi, you can continue north eastwards from here on the track to return to Stazzo di Ziomas and from there to the car park. Otherwise, for Monte Godi, turn sharp right and leave the track to walk south eastwards for 600 metres along the pathless crest, which descends to the lonely **monument stone** at the foot of Monte Godi. ▸

This marks the spot where Pope John Paul II, a noted lover of wild Abruzzo, came to pray in 2003.

From here the Monte Godi extension will add a good two hours to your day, but if you've the time and energy, it's well worth it. If not, go left (north west) from the monument and follow a track to soon rejoin the main route back to Stazzo di Ziomas, and retrace steps from there to the car park.

To ascend Monte Godi, however, continue a little south east from the monument stone, to where the slope of the mountain steepens. A path climbs the slope obliquely rightwards. It continues on a rising contour, through patches of trees, and turns more to the left before entering a small grassy hollow. Climb out the far side and onto the broad ridge. Turn left (north) and walk up the

Monte Godi and the view towards Scanno

stony ridge with trees on the right and a **shepherds' hut** in a hollow on the left.

Keep on a line northwards to reach a sub-peak. The main summit lies about 500 metres away to the north across a large depression. To avoid crossing the depression, take a line north eastwards around its east rim and up to the main ridge that runs eastwards from the summit. Turn left and follow the ridge to the 2011m summit of **Monte Godi**, with its cairn and fluttering metal pennant.

To descend, reverse your steps to the **monument stone** where, rather than bearing left, you should continue on the track north west. The track soon rejoins the main route back to **Stazzo di Ziomas**; from here you can retrace steps to the car park.

WALK 28

Monte Marsicano

Start/finish	Central square, Pescasseroli (41.809097, 13.790461)
Distance	20km
Total ascent/descent	1265m
Difficulty	3 (route probably snowbound from November to May)
Walking time	7hr
High/low points	2245m/1155m
Map	Monti Marsicani (1:25,000)
Access	Pescasseroli is approached on the SS83 along the Upper Sangro valley. (See Appendix B for further details.) There is a regular bus service that connects Pescasseroli and Castel di Sangro.
Parking	From the north-west, there are roadside parking places on the left, along the river, just before the main houses of the village. Walk along the main road to the village centre. From the south east, as the avenue of trees with lawns begins, a left turn leads to a large car park behind the two streets of small houses. It's a short walk to the main square.

A magnificent itinerary linking Pescasseroli with the summit of Monte Marsicano, the keystone of the Abruzzo National Park and a point commanding the entire area. The remote and very beautiful Valle di Corte is climbed to approach the peak via the wild and empty corrie at its head. Descent lingers along the skyline crest before heading down forested slopes and finally across gentle hills and stone-walled pastures to return to the village.

This is a big mountain route – a full day that requires fine weather in order to be accomplished comfortably, especially in the descent from the crest, where the path is briefly non-existent. Finding the way needs good eyesight and the recommended map, and ideally a GPS device (with waypoints loaded) as backup. So pick the right day, know where you are at all times, and enjoy a really wonderful walk that captures everything that is best about the park!

From the north east corner of the square, walk along the main road up the valley for about 60 metres. The historic village centre lies to the left. See a sign to a Tabacchi on the right. Turn right along a cobbled alley called '1 Traverso Sangro' and cross the river. Turn left and walk alongside the right (true left) bank of the river.

In about 500 metres the road becomes an unsealed lane called Via Canale Pratorosso. Continue on, passing a large drinking **fountain** for animals on the right. The lane draws away from the river and bears right to face the forested slopes about 2km ahead.

Follow the lane through fields, passing a **picnic spot** and information board on the right. The lane steepens on entering the gap through the higher ground. Beautiful beech forest closes around; in late summer and autumn logging is often carried out. ▶ The way levels and enters an open area. Fork right at a junction to follow the descending track marked 'A6'. The track swings to the south east (right), leaving you at the entrance to the magnificent **Valle di Corte**.

Logging is a local-scale activity here, with teams of mules used to transport weighty timber loads to the lane – a tradition that stretches back hundreds of years.

The view ahead, across meadows and into thick forest, ends with the northern amphitheatre of the Marsicano massif. Follow the track into the valley and stay in the bottom all the way up. The 4x4 track becomes a mule

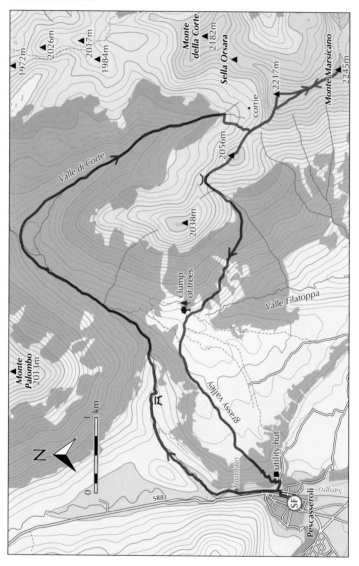

Woodcutter's mules

track, then a path and then a stream bed. The solitude is immense. Find your way through a muddle of boulders and fallen trees. Soon enough you step into the wild corrie. The path climbs glacial moraines on the right (west) to the rim of the amphitheatre. The last stretch zig-zags up scree to pass through a nick in the rock bands.

The view opens out across the Sangro valley and way into Lazio. Turn south east (left) and follow the rim, climbing towards the unnamed peak that dominates the corrie – point 2217m. Halfway up, notice a vague track rising rightwards across the grassy south west flank of the mountain. Follow it to arrive halfway along the ridge between point 2217m and the summit of **Monte Marsicano**, 1km to the south east. Walk easily along the ridge to the cairn at 2245m.

> The whole of the **national park** lies below – the Sangro valley to the south west, the huge corrie to the north east, Monte Petroso away to the south east, and the ridge running north west for 4km.

Return to where you joined the ridge. Then continue along it to point 2217m itself and the fantastic view of Valle di Corte below. ▶ Go carefully down the rim to the nick, where the path drops into the corrie. Do not go

Beyond lies La Terratta and adjacent peaks of the ridge south west of Scanno.

175

The summit of Monte Marsicano

back down, but continue north west on the ridge. Climb to the next high point and then descend to the lowest point of the saddle beyond.

Turn south west (left) and descend grassy slopes on the north west (right) side of the valley. A good path appears, but as trees approach it disappears. There are no markings, so be careful. Go ahead on the right side of the valley bottom. Enter the trees and descend 100m or so, always on the right, looking carefully for signs of a vague mule track that heads away north west (right) on a gently descending traverse. Don't overshoot – carved names on trees and faint paint marks should confirm the line.

The mule track becomes established and paint marks reassuringly clearer as you head through the forest. Gaps in the trees appear, allowing views down into the Valle Filatoppa, which rises from the south east to the valley head, where a flat grassy area and **clump of trees** mark the end of the forest.

Walk beyond the trees, north west, on a 4x4 track across pasture. After about 300 metres it bends sharply right; at this point take a lesser 4x4 track on the left into a shallow **grassy valley** that runs south west, through low hills, towards Pescasseroli. At first, the track descends on the right, then more in the centre, leading finally to another track by an old stone wall on the left. After 2km the little valley meets another arriving from the right, and forest appears ahead.

Cross a broken stone wall and walk to the forest along the continuing valley. The path descends on the right to enter the trees. It becomes an old mule track that zig-zags down to a house near a green **utility hut** and the tarmacked road. Turn right and walk down to the River Sangro. Turn left to find yourself back at the bridge you crossed at the start of the day. Walk along the alley and back into **Pescasseroli** to find a choice of refreshment opportunities.

WALK 29

Colli Alti and Bassi from Pescasseroli

Start/finish	Central square, Pescasseroli (41.809097, 13.790461)
Distance	18.5km
Total ascent/descent	660m
Difficulty	2 (route probably snowbound from November to Easter)
Walking time	6hr
High/low points	1458m/1118m
Map	Monti Marsicani (1:25,000)
Access	Pescasseroli is approached on the SS83 along the Upper Sangro valley. (See Appendix B for further details.) There is a regular bus service that connects Pescasseroli and Castel di Sangro.
Parking	From the north-west, there are roadside parking places on the left, along the river, just before the main houses of the village. Walk along the main road to the village centre. From the south east, as the avenue of trees with lawns begins, a left turn leads to a large car park behind the two streets of small houses. It's a short walk to the main square.

An exploration of the pastures and woodland that lie between the Upper Sangro and Filatoppa valleys. This easygoing circuit takes in the hills above Pescasseroli, the main settlement of the Abruzzo National Park, and extends southwards to Opi, a distinctive and ancient village perched high on a rocky shoulder above the River Sangro. The empty hills offer a silent escape from the relatively busy Sangro valley. Opi, one of the best hilltop villages in Abruzzo, presents opportunities for lunch – as well as the prospect of viewing golden eagles cruising over nearby rocky ridges. This is a day for when the weather or inclination suggests pastoral landscapes and civilisation rather than remote mountaintops.

From the north east corner of the square in **Pescasseroli**, walk along the main road up the valley for about 60 metres. The historic village centre lies to the left. See a sign to a Tabacchi on the right. Turn right along a cobbled alley called '1 Traverso Sangro' and cross the river.

Turn left and walk alongside the right (true left) bank of the river, and after a few metres turn right into a rising tarmacked road with new lamp posts. A faint blue paint flash should be noticeable on the left-hand wall. At the end of the sealed road, turn left on to a stony lane at a green **utility hut** with meters.

View south east from the Colli Alti, with Monte Marsicano on the left

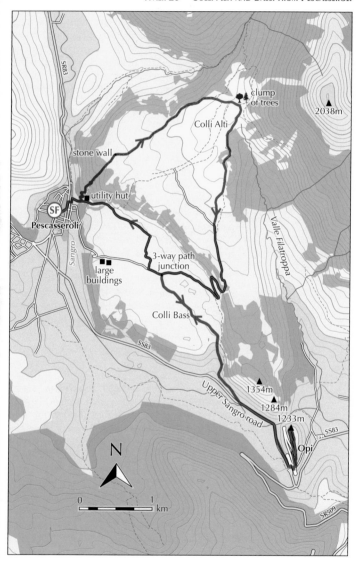

There are occasional
paint flashes
on the trees.

Pass behind houses and start up a fine old mule track that zig-zags through the pine forest. ◀ Emerge into a slight valley that runs ahead, north east, to a low **stone wall** where the valley splits. Take the right fork that swings east, but then resumes climbing north east through the soft pasture land of the **Colli Alti**. Follow the ancient lane through the valley, crossing to the left and skirting woods before reaching a larger 4x4 track that rises from the left. Turn right and walk south east along the track to a **clump of trees** and flat turfy area at the head of Valle Filatroppa.

The wonderful view opens out – Opi stands in the middle distance, perched on a promontory. Do not follow the blue-waymarked path on the left (which leads to the summit of Marsicano), but walk south across level ground. Don't descend into the valley; skirt its head, keeping roughly level, and follow the developing path into the woods and meadows to the right side of the valley. The way is marked with occasional posts.

In the first edition of this guide the route description did, in fact, descend the **Valle Filatroppa** to Opi. It may still just be possible for the intrepid, but the path has fallen into very poor condition and markers are almost non-existent. Whether by design or neglect, the park authorities are no longer encouraging this way.

Continue following the path southwards, across meadows and through small stands of trees, looking out for the infrequent marker posts. The path becomes a 4x4 track and remains on a level course across the grassland. ◀ The track descends to lower meadows, the Colli Bassi, via three hairpins and now heads north west across flat grassland towards Pescasseroli. The rooves of the large buildings of a tourist complex appear ahead before you arrive at a signposted **three-way path junction**.

The beautiful vista
ahead includes
Monte Petroso and
Monte La Meta, with
Monte Marsicano
on the left.

If you want to cut the route short and save a couple of hours, you could continue towards the buildings and then to Pescasseroli, omitting Opi – see the latter part of the route description from the three-way path junction.

However, for Opi, turn left at the junction (signed 'E2 Pietre Bianche') and head south east past the small fields and across the soft pasture to enter a small, open valley. The path continues through the tightening valley, whose sides are partially wooded, before beginning to descend.

A fence is crossed and the path drops obliquely to reach the **Upper Sangro road**. Walk left along the road,

Opi church

mindful of passing cars. The meadows of the valley lie to your right and steep hillside to your left; the village of Opi appears, perched on the promotory at the end of the hillside. The road passes over the Sangro river before reaching a pedestrian crossing point below the village.

Ascend steps on the left (east) that cut across the hairpins of the village access road. Follow pathways and alleys into the houses to reach the hotel and restaurant, La Pieja, and **Opi**'s main street, which runs up to the church and the museum behind it. ◀

The Upper Sangro valley stretches either way from the ridge, while the river itself pours through the little gorge behind.

> The **memorial** at the beautiful viewpoint halfway up the street serves as a reminder of a very dark day in World War II when the British bombed Opi in the mistaken belief that German troops were occupying the village. There were many civilian casualties.

After exploring the village, find your way back to the steps and descend to the **Upper Sangro road**. Turn right and retrace your route all the way back to the signposted **three-way path junction**, and from there turn left towards the buildings and Pescasseroli.

The 4x4 track continues north west. However, after 200 metres turn right on a further 4x4 track that heads across meadows towards a bank of trees. This track swings left to descend gently north west, reaching the point where the ascent on the mule track began at the beginning of the day. Go down the hill to the river. Turn left to return to the bridge you crossed earlier. Walk along the alley and into **Pescasseroli**.

SULMONA VALLEY
AND MONTE GENZANA

The forest road between Pettorano and Monte Genzana (Walk 32)

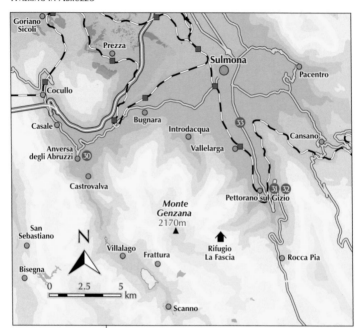

WALK 30

Anversa degli Abruzzi and Castrovalva

Start/finish	Opposite L'Angolo delle Grazie café in main piazza, Anversa degli Abruzzi (41.994399, 13.803494)
Distance	7km
Total ascent/descent	555m
Difficulty	1 (route snowbound for some of the winter)
Walking time	3hr
High/low points	834m/511m
Map	Monte Genzana, Monte Rotella (1:25,000)
Access	From Sulmona, take the well-signposted road (SR479) for Scanno, passing turn-offs first for Introdaqua and

| | then Bugnara before reaching Anversa after about 14km. You can also reach Anversa by taking the Cocullo junction from the A25 motorway: turn left at the end of the motorway access road before passing through the village of Casale to reach Anversa, about 4km from the motorway. From Scanno, take the SR479, passing through the Sagittario gorge. |
| **Parking** | Near the post office on the road to Scanno. (There is no parking on the piazza.) From Sulmona, drive through the narrow village centre to reach the post office. |

This delightfully varied round trip links two fine ancient villages at the northern end of the 9km Sagittario gorge, which separates the northern massifs of the Abruzzo National Park to the south west from Monte Genzana to the east. The climb from Anversa degli Abruzzi, recognised as one of the most beautiful villages in the region, through native woodlands, is steep but over quickly. This allows a leisurely stroll into Castrovalva, a much smaller settlement situated in a remarkable location along a narrow ridge above the gorge. A descent into the gorge and amble through its rocky depths soon returns you to the welcome cafés of Anversa.

Descend behind the chestnut trees down paths and alleyways to where the Sagittario river is diverted into a fast-flowing irrigation canal. Cross the river to Anversa's little **botanical garden**. ▶ Locate a sign pointing left for Castrovalva at the corner of a small yard. (You will see signs too for the Sentiero Geologico, which the route is also called.)

This charming spot is full of information on the local flora and archaeology.

Go left along the side of the yard, and at its end follow the old mule track steeply upwards to the right through woods to pass beneath a noticeable rocky bluff. Emerge on top at a splendid **viewpoint**. The path climbs for about 10min more before reaching an inter-section with a larger track and a signpost. Continue, keeping right (south east) along the undulating track, and gradually draw level with Castrovalva across the rising valley.

185

Pass the **cemetery** and join the tarmac road. Head further up the valley for a few hundred metres before turning right for the gentle rise to **Castrovalva**. At the junction of the road that ascends from the Sagittario gorge, there is a plaque.

> In 1930, from this spot, the Dutch artist **Escher** made a lithograph called 'Castrovalva', which now hangs in the Museum of National Art in Washington. (You can see it at www.nga.gov – search for Castrovalva.) Little seems to have changed in the intervening 90 years – the A25 motorway clinging to the mountainside beyond Anversa and the wind farm above being the only obvious differences.

A café may be open in summer months near the post office.

Pass into the small central piazza. ◀ Continue to the end of the village, taking a lane on the left. Drop down steps beyond the last house and onto the narrow ridge. The Sagittario gorge lies 200m below on the left. Walk along to a point just before the black metal cross where the track zig-zags down left. (Continuing beyond

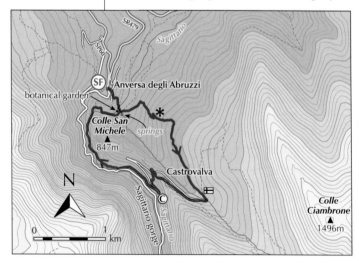

Castrovalva

the communications mast to the chapel is a worthwhile diversion, but you will need to return to the cross.)

The old mule track passes above the road tunnel and, after a few descending turns, joins the road itself. Turn left and follow it down.

At the hairpin bend it is worth clambering into the **cave**. Your eyes will soon adjust to notice the remnants of stalactite curtains above.

Continue down to the main road. Just before the junction take the path on the right for the lovely section between the steep cliffs of the **Sagittario gorge**.

The path loses height as you pass though the narrow valley, switching banks as the encroaching cliffs force changes of direction. ▶ Large boulders lie strewn along the floor, including some cast down from excavations of the road above. The cold waters rush between tight narrows and plunge into eroded pools. Soon the gorge opens, and the first smallholdings of Anversa are reached.

On a hot day the shade is delicious.

Follow the level track as it nears Anversa. Turn right at the first obvious opportunity and go back to the river. Go left before crossing back into the **botanical garden**. The visitor centre, housed in an old water works, may be open, and the **springs** that swell the Sagittario river are always flowing. Retrace the path up into **Anversa** and to the piazza.

WALK 31
Monte Mattone from Pettorano sul Gizio

Start/finish	Piazza at the lower entrance archway to the village of Pettorano (41.975453, 13.958401)
Distance	12.5km
Total ascent/descent	1030m
Difficulty	2 (route snowbound for some of the winter)
Walking time	4hr 30min
High/low points	1515m/560m
Map	Monte Genzana, Monte Rotella (1:25,000)
Access	Pettorano sul Gizio lies at the far south eastern end of the Sulmona valley, just off the SS17 main road to Roccaraso and Napoli and about 10km from Sulmona itself. From Sulmona, take the first turn off the SS17 for Pettorano on the right. The road then takes three hairpins as it climbs to the village proper.
Parking	Road or piazza at the bottom of the village, next to the small park

A strenuous but rewarding expedition in the Monte Genzana and Alto Gizio nature reserve from delightful Pettorano sul Gizio, situated on an elevated ridge at the south eastern end of the Sulmona valley. This provides a perfect introduction to the higher mountains of Abruzzo and a good test of fitness! The route starts and finishes in the old village and takes in two silent wooded valleys descending from Monte Genzana, plus an ascent of Monte Mattone, a sub-peak of Genzana affording a magnificent panorama of south central Abruzzo. A busy half-day!

Pettorano sul Gizio is one of the most attractive villages in Abruzzo – a deserved member of the restoration and promotion organisation I Borghi più Belli d'Italia ('Italy's most Beautiful Villages'). Situated on an elevated ridge at the south eastern end of the Sulmona valley, it is a peaceful and ancient place

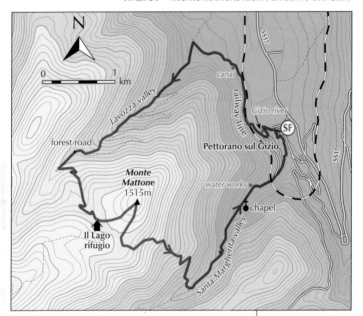

overlooking the entrance to forested valleys that run
deep into the Genzana massif.

From the piazza, walk back round the hairpin and down
the road for 50 metres. Go down steps on the left and
follow the path back left behind houses to the church on
the first hairpin. Go left down a side road signposted for
the nature reserve and past the old *polizia* building. Cross
the **Gizio river** and straight away take the cycle path on
the right.

After about 300 metres, turn up left under the **railway
line** and then climb above it. Follow the path alongside
the line, with the cutting wall on your left, then swing
leftwards and up to a lane. Just before the lane, cross the
swirling **canal** that feeds captured waters of the Gizio to
the irrigation channels fanning out across the southern
Sulmona valley.

Pettorano sits in a peaceful location among olive groves and orchards

Fork left and follow the lane as it rises towards the Lavozza valley. In about 500 metres the lane ends at the junction with a forest road coming up from the right. Turn left and enter the **valley**. The road rises steadily and the forested sides draw together. After another 800 metres or so, the path leaves the road and continues straight ahead (right) along the bottom of the valley, following occasional markers. Rise steadily until you turn left to climb the valley side steeply and rejoin the **forest road**.

Go left up an ancient lane through a beautiful beech forest before emerging onto a high grazed meadow. This is the broad saddle between the summit of Mattone on the left and the long, wide ridge descending from the summit of Genzana to the right (see Walk 32). Reach the **Il Lago rifugio** and then cross the meadow behind it, going steeply up to the 1515m **Monte Mattone** summit in a direct line. Flop on the turfy top and enjoy the magnificent views.

Return to the saddle, aiming for the lowest point on the left (south east), where a vague track enters the forest on the steep sides of the Santa Margherita valley. Descend through the woods for a delightful 40min or so on a clear and well-graded old mule track, eventually reaching the white 4x4 road in the bottom of the **valley**.

Turn left and amble along the descending lane through the glorious valley back to the village. Pass the isolated Santa Margherita **chapel** and picnic spot (where water may be available) and, a little further on, a small archaeological site.

The approach to Pettorano is heralded by the **water works** at the source of the Gizio river, where much of the flow is diverted for the irrigation system. Pass under the railway viaduct before ascending lanes and steps to **Pettorano**'s historic village centre. ▶ The start point is further north west along the village spine.

Wonderful Piazza Zannelli hosts a bar, small shop, the reserve information centre and, far from least, Il Torchio restaurant.

WALK 32
Monte Genzana from Pettorano sul Gizio

Start/finish	Piazza at the lower entrance archway to the village of Pettorano (41.975453, 13.958401)
Distance	20km
Total ascent/descent	1750m
Difficulty	3 (route probably snowbound from November to Easter)
Walking time	7hr 30min
High/low points	2170m/562m
Map	Monte Genzana, Monte Rotella (1:25,000)
Access	Pettorano sul Gizio lies at the far south eastern end of the Sulmona valley, just off the SS17 main road to Roccaraso and Napoli and about 10km from Sulmona itself. From Sulmona, take the first turn off the SS17 for Pettorano on the right. The road then takes three hairpins as it climbs to the village proper.
Parking	Road or piazza at the bottom of the village, next to the small park

An ascent of a 'keystone' peak within the ranges south of Sulmona. The route, entirely within the Monte Genzana and Alto Gizio nature reserve, takes a largely direct valley approach from Pettorano and returns along a broad grassy shoulder before descending forested slopes back to the delightful village. Route markings are inconsistent and poor in places, and care needs to be taken picking the right path on the descent ridge beyond the La Fascia rifugio, but you'll be following major topographical features and on a clear day there are few navigational concerns.

Start early: this is a full and varied day with views that will linger long in the memory and an ascent that will linger long in the legs! And tread quietly: you've a chance of spotting deer, wild boar, and possibly even the recently returned wolf.

Boasting two bars, a shop, post office, chemist and two great restaurants, **Pettorano sul Gizio** really deserves its billing as 'one of the most beautiful villages in Italy'. The information centre for the Riserva Monte Genzana is up the steps on Piazza Zanelli. If it's open, pick up a free copy of their map of the reserve.

From the piazza, walk back round the hairpin and down the road for 50 metres. Go down steps on the left and follow the path back left behind houses to the church on the first hairpin. Go left down a side road signposted for the nature reserve and past the old *polizia* building.

Arrive at the Gizio river and turn left into the archeolgical park that lies along the bottom of the valley. (If the park is closed, continue along the road to the railway viaduct.) Walk through the pretty park, past recently restored watermill buildings, and find a way out at the far end via a vague path up onto the road on the right. Follow the road to the **railway viaduct**.

Pass under the viaduct and head up the 4x4 track into the valley, passing rocky outcrops among the trees on either side. The source of the Gizio appears on the right, harnessed within the structures of the irrigation scheme that feeds its waters to the fertile valley between

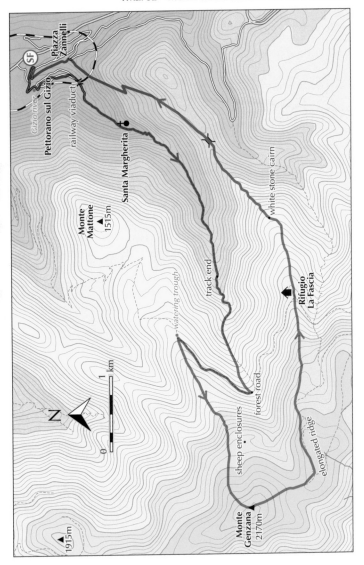

Watering trough on the grassy ridge

Pettorano and Sulmona. Soon reach the solitary little church of **Santa Margherita** and an outdoor classroom.

Climb steadily up the valley, passing the junction with a cross-path. The peace and quiet is overwhelming but occasionally shattered by a woodpecker or jay. Find your rhythm as the valley sides draw closer and the kilometres fall behind. After about a further hour, reach the **track end** – a path leads into the upper reaches of the valley.

Follow the narrow path, sometimes twisting and faint, as the gradient steepens. You'll soon find your way blocked by the extensive debris of broken trees, brought down by an avalanche several years ago. Go to the right of the debris and pick your own way further up the valley, keeping the tumble of twisted wood on your left, to reach a **forest road**. Turn right and walk along the mercifully level and well-graded road for 1km until you reach an animal **watering trough** on the open grassy ridge between the Valle Margherita and the Val Lavozza.

Turn sharp left at the trough and begin to climb directly up the broad ridge towards the summit of Monte Genzana, identifiable on the skyline by the communications mast just to its left. The way is on an easy 4x4 track, which then becomes a footpath used by grazing cattle.

The climb is constant but steady. Continue up between a small crag on your right and, on your left, old stone **sheep enclosures** on a saddle between an outlying top and the summit mound of Monte Genzana ahead. There is now no distinct path. It is easiest to skirt the depression below the summit to the right (north) and then approach it along the right-hand skyline.

The cairn on the **Monte Genzana** summit is daubed with possibly useful arrows pointing towards Pettorano, Intradaqua and Frattura. Unmistakable is the mast which, mercifully, wasn't put right on the top.

> **Monte Genzana** and its subsidiary tops dominate the skyline south of Sulmona. At 2170m, its rounded grassy summit provides a wonderful panorama in all directions and an especially full view to the north – Sulmona, the Peligna valley and the Gran Sasso peaks forming the skyline beyond. It's a wide, open place – the high point of a ridge running south east towards Roccaraso and the mountains above Lago Barrea in the Abruzzo National Park. Frattura and Scanno lie below the south west flank, offering an alternative descent to anyone who doesn't want or need to return to Pettorano.

When you have taken in the wonderful views, look beyond the mast to the south east and locate a distinct, low and elongated crag about 500 metres away. Walk down, across a small saddle and up to the right-hand end of the crag. Turn left and head east along the top of the edge until it peters out after a few hundred metres. You are now on the rounded descent ridge, with the tree-filled valley you so recently sweated up visible way down on the left. This is a glorious, open space where you can gaze on the long skyline ridge culminating in Monte Rottello on the other side of the Cinquemiglia plain.

Go down, keeping reasonably close to the left of the ridge. After about 1km, scrubby trees appear and the path dips in and out of beech woods spilling up from the valleys on either side. Descend more steeply to a meadow

*Descending from
Monte Genzana*

where **Rifugio La Fascia** lies beyond a forest road; Pettorano but a few hours further on.

The path crosses the meadow, following occasional poles, until it descends into the patchy trees ahead. The path is indistinct and markings very few (the waymarks on a GPS might be useful if you have the means). Take care to keep on the crest and out of the trees on the left.

Pass through a band of trees and cross a final open area with medium-height juniper shrubs, walking towards a conspicuous **white stone cairn** at the edge of the forest, ahead and to the left. From the cairn the path plunges left into wonderful beech woods and starts to lose height.

Zig-zag steeply down through the fallen leaves of many past autumns until Pettorano appears in view. Soon reach a little **saddle** and viewpoint with a sign pointing back to the rifugio, and where the cross-path drops to the valley floor. Continue to descend an old mule path at an acceptable angle, the path becoming ever wider and more defined until, in another couple of kilometres, **Pettorano** is upon you.

Turn left and enter the village's upper end. The Locanda bar and restaurant may prove irresistible, but wander further on, past the castle and down the main street to the delightful Piazza Zannelli with its bar, excellent restaurant, shop and a wonderful view back up the valley you ascended. Continue into Piazza Umberto 1 and follow alleys back to the start.

WALK 33

A tour of the Valle del Gizio

Start/finish	Tamoil garage on the SS17, about 2km south of Sulmona (42.017448, 13.942652)
Distance	17.5km
Total ascent/descent	805m
Difficulty	2; or 1 if omitting Colle Mitra. (Colle Mitra likely to be snowbound in winter months.)
Walking time	6hr
High/low points	1067m/461m
Map	Monte Genzana, Monte Rotella (1:25,000)
Access	The Valle del Gizio is a few kilometres south east of Sulmona. The SS17 runs right through it. From the centre of Sulmona, head south east following signs for Roccaraso and Napoli. You will join the SS17 main road (that bypasses Sulmona). Turn south east (right) onto the main road and follow it until you reach the Tamoil petrol station and café on the left. From the south east (Roccaraso), take the SS17 and Tamoil is on the right about 6km beyond the turning for Pettorano.
Parking	Outside the café

An excursion around the wide Valle del Gizio at the far south eastern end of the broad and fertile Sulmona basin, which marks the confluence of three rivers – the Sagittario, the Aterno and the Gizio. This easily accessed route follows lanes through fields and vineyards on the flat valley floor and then olive groves on the slopes to reach the beautiful old village of Pettorano. Return from the village is best accomplished via a climb up to Colle Mitra, which overlooks the whole of the Sulmona basin. (This climb and the final descent are steep, across pathless mountainside. You will need good footwear and should take water.) The view is very much worth the effort, but a return along the valley floor is an option for a far less taxing day.

The **Valle del Gizio** runs south east for about 8km from Sulmona until closed in by mountains and the pass onto the high Cinquemiglia plain. It's a place of old farming hamlets, scattered vineyards, cereal fields and orchards, hemmed with olive groves, into which Sulmona's villa belt is only slowly beginning to encroach.

From the Tamoil garage, cross the road and go left for 100 metres to a right turn for Val Pescara. (Take care as there is no footpath.) Go down the slope, heading left past houses, to the valley bottom and cross the **Gizio** – no more than a small stream in the summer. Go up to a crossroads and turn left. In 30 metres, beyond the little **school**, turn right and walk through the houses of the old farming hamlet ahead. ◀ At a T-junction, turn left and then join Via Case La Rocca – one of the main lanes through the valley.

The alternative return route, avoiding Colle Mitra, rejoins the main route at this point.

Walk south east for about 1.5km, continuing past a right turn where there are dog kennels. Reach a **black walnut grove** on the right and turn right. The road leads, in a large 'S', to the bricked-up **Vallelarga station**. Cross the track and turn left. In 100 metres go left again, then in another 250 metres turn right up a little lane to the main road.

Turn right, then quickly take the first left. Climb the slope to a junction with a **water trough** on the left. Continue climbing the hillside, through olive groves, to reach a T-junction. Go left and more steeply upwards until the road ends at an **abandoned farmhouse** – the highest in the valley.

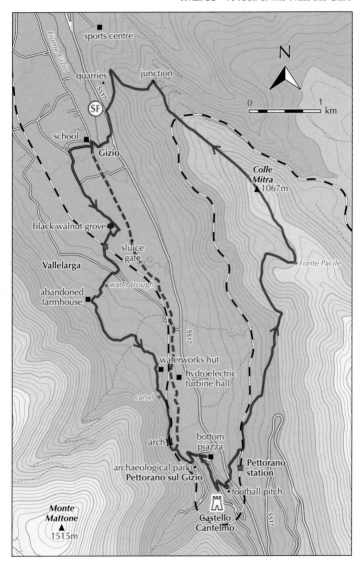

At the farmhouse, go left on a level track which quickly turns right to a junction. Go left on a slightly undulating 4x4 track that leads gloriously through trees, heading south east. The track ends at the partially concreted road into Val Lavozza that rises from the left. Turn right, and then immediately turn left down a 4x4 track that continues south east towards Pettorano. After 450 metres pass a concete **waterworks hut** on the left, and soon after reach a track junction.

Turn left, downhill, to cross the **canal** that feeds the waters of the Gizio into the valley's irrigation network. Follow the path to find yourself above the railway line as Pettorano comes into view.

> The picturesque **mountain railway** linking Sulmona with Castel di Sangro runs to the far end of the valley before turning back to climb the steep north eastern flank below the strategic hill of Colle Mitra. The SS17 'Abruzzo highway' also runs through and climbs stilted hairpins to gain the high plain.

The path runs alongside the line then descends beneath an **arch** to the cycle path. Turn right and walk to the road below Pettorano. Opposite is the entrance to the **archaeological park**; if it is open, go in to see the fine restored watermills, but then return to walk up the road, via hairpins, to the **bottom piazza** of the village. ◄

A small park offers a commanding view north over the whole of the valley.

Go through the arch and find your way, via steps and alleys, to beautiful Piazza Zannelli in the historical centre of **Pettorano sul Gizio**. Continue your exploration along the spine of the village to the castle, **Castello Cantelmo**.

For the easy return, which should take about 1hr 30min, retrace your steps to go back along the cycle path to the junction with the path down from the arch. Don't go up it but continue alongside the river to a **hydroelectric turbine hall**. Go on past a reservoir (empty) on the right to reach the road. Go left along the road for 100 metres, and before another railway arch turn right down an unsealed road which soon forks. Take the left fork and walk down the lane. After about 1.4km, keep right at a

fork with a sluice gate, and continue all the way back to the school building. From here, retrace your steps to the start.

Alternatively, if you relish a challenge and a glorious view, from the castle return slightly towards Piazza Zannelli and then find a way down narrow steets and steps on the right to the road that skirts the village on the east side. Cross over and continue down Via Vittorio Monaco towards the **football pitch**. Before reaching the pitch, turn left up to the main road.

Cross over and go up the road signposted for **Pettorano station**. Where the road swings right, go through a tunnel under the railway line and turn left onto an unsealed track. After 400 metres keep left to continue rising gently – don't go sharp right up the steep hill. At a fork, keep right – do not continue alongside the railway track. ▸

The old 4x4 track leads across the hillside, through patchy woodland, rising gently for about 1.8km until it ends in the bottom of the valley that leads up into an

Summer in the Valle del Gizio

GPS waypoints would be useful for this section (but not essential).

amphitheatre on the right. From this point there is no path until you reach Fonte Pacile.

Cross the valley bed and begin going left and upwards, making a steeply rising traverse around the outside of the open hillside. As you climb and turn the hillside, a dip in the skyline appears ahead – aim for it. The going is hard work. At the skyline the ground becomes easier. Head right along vague sheep tracks towards the clump of trees about 300 metres away, which is **Fonte Pacile** with drinking water.

From the fountain go north west (left) on a level path across the hillside to a path junction. From here follow the ridge (there are wheel tracks) up to the giant iron cross on **Colle Mitra** (1067m). The view down to Sulmona and across the basin is tremendous – worth every drop of sweat!

Descend the ridge north west from the cross. After passing trees on the right the path bears left to join a larger one ascending from Sulmona. Turn right onto it and pass over the entrance to a railway tunnel. Descend towards Sulmona sports centre. At a signed **junction**, turn left onto a side path and descend to cross the small valley.

The path climbs and leads on, beneath power lines, towards old **quarries**. At a junction above the quarry, turn left. The path swings back left and descends obliquely out onto the hillside. At a hairpin back right, leave the path and take a direct line to the Tamoil garage (café) plainly visible below. Take care on the steep scree. There is no path.

Cross the irrigation canal by a green bridge behind the garage. With luck, the café will still be open!

THE SIRENTE-VELINO
REGIONAL PARK

Valle d'Arano (Walk 35)

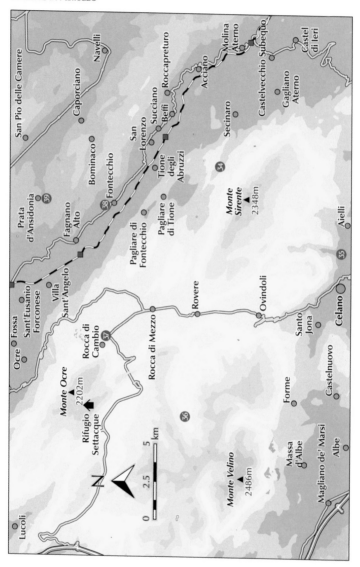

WALK 34
Monte Sirente

Start/finish	Chalet Sirente rifugio between Secinaro and Rocca di Mezzo (42.160623, 13.636185)
Distance	9.5km
Total ascent/descent	1155m
Difficulty	3 (route likely to be snowbound between November and May)
Walking time	6hr
High/low points	2348m/1186m
Map	Velino-Sirente (1:25,000)
Access	Chalet Sirente is 7km from Secinaro and 13km from Rocca di Mezzo in the heart of the Sirente-Velino Park. It is in the forest about 2km south east of the high plain of Prati dei Sirente. Rocca di Mezzo is most easily reached from L'Aquila in the north and Celano and Ovindoli in the south, while from the Sulmona basin or the Adriatic coast the best approach is from Secinaro (reached via the Aterno gorge or valley and then the Subequo valley).
Parking	The rifugio is on the left as you approach from Secinaro. There is parking on the other side of the road.

Although the Sirente-Velino has only regional park status, it is the equal of the national parks in magnificence, access, protection and wilderness. This, the 'via normale' to 2348m Monte Sirente, offers a surprisingly direct route from deep beech forest to the summit. From below, the north east wall of the mountain looks daunting, rising straight up from the high plain of Prati dei Sirente, but the way skirts the steeper sections on a spectacular outing into wild country. The view from the top over the Sirente meadow is equally impressive. The big wall means return by the same route is the only real option for a day trip (unless you can arrange to finish at Rovere at the north west end of the Sirente ridge). Gazing back to the summit at the end of the day and seeing what you've achieved is a great satisfaction.

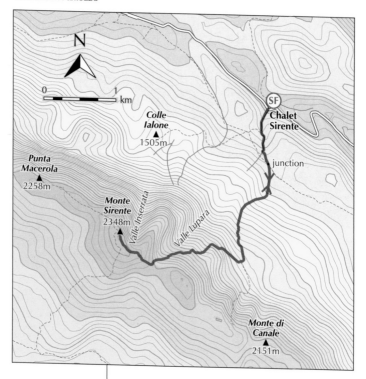

This point is also known as Fonte all' Aqua.

Start from the right of the rifugio as you face it. ◀ A 4x4 track leads into the trees. The route is marked with red-and-white paint splashes and occasionally numbered '15'. The words 'Sirente' or 'Lupara' are occasionally painted on trees or rocks.

Go up past a green building and arrive at a junction with the well-signposted bridle path that passes along the foot of the Sirente wall. Keep left, following the bridle path for about 200 metres, before the route to Sirente forks right to ascend through woods. Watch carefully for this **junction**.

The way soon establishes itself as a fine old mule-track that zigs-zags up through the mixed forest, steeply at times, until swinging to the south east (left) and climbing more easily to the tree line.

On emerging onto the meadow between the forest and the broken cliffs above, the path swings north west (right) to ascend the slopes. The way is well graded and bears right, crossing rocky shoulders as it gains height before entering the left-hand side (true right) of the barren **Valle Lupara**. The path runs onwards, contouring neatly, to the col at the head of the steep rocky valley. As it approaches the headwall it steepens – the last 100 metres to the crest are the most energetic of the day.

Once on the crest the huge view south west opens up – down across pastoral slopes to the Celano gorge, with the prominent Serra di Celano behind and, further still, the flat Fucino basin. This side of the mountain is a complete contrast to the way you have come. The view back is equally impressive.

Turn north west (right) and follow the rising crest line easily to the summit cross on **Monte Sirente** about 500 metres further on. The path skirts the head of the very steep Valle Inserrata. Impressive cliffs on either side feel like a funnel to suck in the unwary.

Leaving the forest on Monte Sirente

Entering Valle Lupara

The **view** from the summit is magnificent, particularly to the north east – the meadow of the Prati dei Sirente lies over 1200m below your feet, the semi-abandoned summer shepherds' village of Pagliare di Tione lies beyond, and the peaks of Corno Grande and the Gran Sasso stand on the horizon. Monte Velino stands 20km to the west.

There is no practical way to return to the rifugio other than to retrace your steps. The vague and intimidatingly steep path down the Valle Inserrata is an option, but it is unpleasant going, albeit through impressive scenery. The path in the forest below is indistinct and not well marked. Much better to reverse the via normale.

Alternatively, if you manage to arrange things so that you can finish your day at Rovere, the village at the north west end of the Sirente crest, then the 7km of steady descent along the escarpment makes a great traverse of the mountain.

WALK 35

The Celano gorge via Fonte degli Innamorati

Start/finish	Southern entrance to the Celano gorge, 2km east of Celano (42.085686, 13.567758)
Distance	10.5km
Total ascent/descent	1155m
Difficulty	2 (route flooded winter to May)
Walking time	5hr 30min (3hr if you turn around at Fonte degli Innamorati)
High/low points	1376m/806m
Map	Velino-Sirente (1:25,000)
Access	From Pescara, Sulmona and Rome, take the A25 motorway. Leave at the Aielli–Celano exit and turn right onto the SS5 for 400 metres before turning right for Celano. Pass under the motorway and over the railway. After 400 metres there is a large restaurant on the left before the road bends left (over a little river). Immediately after the bend take a narrow side road on the right that should be signposted 'la foce'. This lane almost doubles back before leading, in 1.5km, to the car park at the gorge entrance. If approaching from Celano town centre, look for the narrow road to 'la foce' on the left just before the main road swings right.
Parking	Car park at entrance to the gorge

An exploration of the Celano gorge, one of the best and most easily accessed of the region's canyons, is a classic Abruzzo day out. Only accessible in the dry summer and autumn months, the route along the deeply incised riverbed leads to the little waterfall and picnic spot of Fonte degli Innamorati. Some may choose to turn around here, but the path can be followed to the top of the gorge, 6km north of Celano, where it opens onto the high plain of Valle d'Arano (recommended not least for the seasonal café set up in a small shepherds' shelter). The gorge is awesome – an exciting and wild place entirely within the regional park. It is full of butterflies in summer, with vultures and golden eagles often soaring high above.

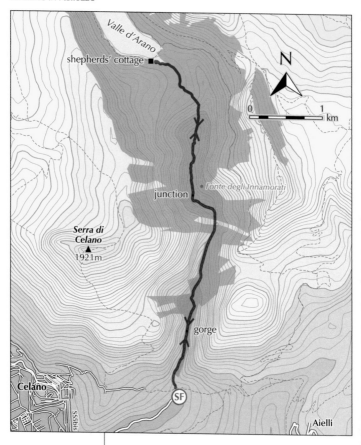

From the car park, head into the gorge beyond the information board. The path crosses a meadow before climbing into pines on the left. A good indication of whether the gorge is passable is if there is water in the riverbed (which you have crossed twice already) – **if there's more than a trickle, it's probably not passable**. Continue in trees above the river until the path drops back to the bed and the first short, narrow section of the **gorge**. ◀

If you can't get through without wet feet, it is probably not worth continuing, as the gorge will be impassable higher up.

If you get through, then the path quits the bed again and takes to trees on the left. Continue without any real possibility of going wrong for about 2.5km until you reach the **junction** and path on the right for the Fonte degli Innamorati. Along this memorable stretch the way, in forest shade, passes continually from one side of the course to the other, and when the walls close spectacularly tight it follows the rocky riverbed itself.

The side track to the **fonte** runs a few hundred metres along the right of the river. In the summer the small cascade pouring from the vegetated overhang may be the only water you will encounter all day. Take a break and feel its refreshing spray.

The depths of the Celano gorge

If the fonte was your goal, retrace your steps to the car park. Otherwise, back at the junction with the main path, turn right and climb through the woods on the left (true right) side of the gorge. The path, less distinct now, crosses a number of rocky areas between pine stands as the riverbed falls away below. It then steepens and zig-zags. ◄ Finally, the gradient lessens and the way straightens though atmospheric, silent forest.

Wonderful views appear back down the gorge.

In 500 metres, the trees thin as the top of the gorge arrives. A magnificent view opens across the grassy Valle d'Arano, and the path joins the white road that runs up from Ovindoli. If you are lucky, the seasonal café in the **shepherds' cottage** to the left will be open for a drink and simple meal. When you are ready, retrace your steps for a second encounter with the gorge and return to the car park.

WALK 36
Monte Velino

Start/finish	Capo Pezza, at the western end of the Piano di Pezza plain (42.182359, 13.428150)
Distance	20km
Total ascent/descent	1515m
Difficulty	3 (route snowbound from November to May)
Walking time	7hr 30min
High/low points	2486m/1532m
Map	Velino-Sirente (1:25,000)
Access	The Piano di Pezza is approached directly from the large village of Rocca di Mezzo, in the heart of the park. Rocca di Mezzo is reached from L'Aquila in the north, via Fossa and Rocca di Cambio, and from Celano in the south, via Ovindoli. It can also be reached from Secinaro to the south east. (For further details see Appendix B.)
Parking	Grassy area at the end of the unsealed road, just before the trees. (If the road feels too rough you could walk from the new rifugio, but it would add at least 2hr to the day.)

One of the finest mountain excursions in Abruzzo and probably the best in the Velino massif. Monte Velino is the highest point in the west of Abruzzo and in the Sirente-Velino Regional Park. But far more, it's the culmination of a wonderful sub-alpine environment – a wild, unspoilt place to thrill anyone lucky enough to visit.

The ascent to the commanding 2486m summit, a guardian of the high Apennines, is a beautifully balanced mix of parkland, forest, sub-alpine meadow, rocky ridges and cols, and a final haul up the summit block. The view from the top is well worth the substantial effort. The recommended descent allows a rest at Rifugio Sebastiani before a relaxing final stretch in the forest. On a clear day this walk will be a well-remembered treasure.

Walk ahead to a fork. Take the right-hand path, sign-posted for Colle dell'Orso and numbered '1', into the trees. The way climbs gently through the beech forest. The tree line is soon reached, with the marvellous grassy corrie at the head of Valle Cerchiata. A **junction** lies 100 metres ahead. The right-hand path leads to Rifugio Sebastiani (numbered '1A'). However, stay left (for Colle dell'Orso), continuing into the corrie. The path ascends the screes of the headwall, first rising left across a rockier band and then, from a grassy promontory, right towards the low saddle on the skyline.

Piano di Pezza

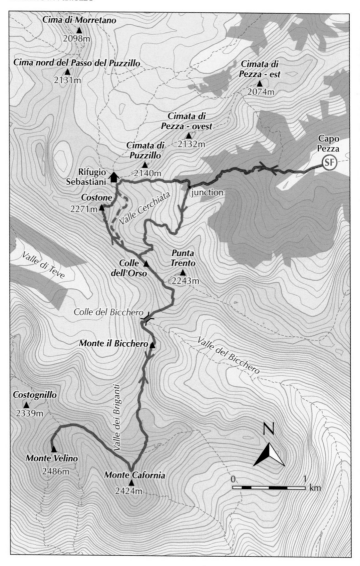

The magnificent **view** from the crest appears – the deep and narrow, thickly forested Valle di Teve to the right and the wide, wild amphitheatre of the Valle dei Briganti at its head to the left. The summit of Monte Velino stands above all other points on the rim of the corrie opposite.

Turn south east (left) and follow the level path along the crest, beyond the summit of **Colle dell'Orso**, to the junction just before Punta Trento (point **2243m**). Turn southwards (to the right) and descend a depression and then grassy slopes to the saddle of **Colle del Bicchero** below – the watershed between Valle di Teve and the Valle del Bicchero that falls to the south east (left).

Climb the grassy slope on the other side to follow the undulating path southwards, skirting the low summit of **Monte il Bicchero**, and then continue almost level for 1km towards the headwall of the main corrie. The path crosses scree and then climbs it, rightwards, to a low point on the left of the skyline. A huge vista opens out, this time to the south across the Fucino basin. Turn south west and follow the path to the 2424m summit of **Monte Cafornia**. Reach a small saddle just behind the main ridge that leads to the outlying summit of Pizzo Cafornia with its prominent cross. ▶

A 20min diversion will take you to the cross and back.

Follow the level path north west, mostly left of the crest but sometimes on it, towards the looming summit of Monte Velino 1km away. The views to either side are wonderful. Velino lies isolated, just back (south west) from the crest. Reach the point below the summit block and turn south west (left) to climb steeply up loose scree to the cross at the top of 2486m **Monte Velino**.

The **view** is immense. The Fucino basin, in the middle distance, lies 1800m below. In the far south lie all of the peaks of the Abruzzo National Park, and to the south west is the Simbruini group. North, across the lonely corrie, is Monte Costone. The weather, hopefully, will allow lunch on the summit.

The approach to Monte Velino

To descend, reverse the route to the saddle at Colle dell'Orso where the crest was first joined. From here a decision is needed – whether to go directly down the way you came, or whether, at the cost of an extra hour, to visit Rifugio Sebastiani. In order to reach the rifugio, a further choice is needed – whether to climb the beckoning Monte Costone and then descend to the rifugio, or whether to cut directly across the east face on a level path to reach it. The latter avoids the last big effort of the day at the cost of possibly the best view.

For the east face traverse, take either of two narrow, unmarked paths that cross the face just beyond the saddle. Both reach the far side at the same height they started. From here continue easily to the **rifugio** and pick up the route description in the final paragraph below.

Alternatively, **for the high route**, climb the ridge steeply to the summit of **Costone**. The path becomes intermittent. The best line is a little back (left) of the crest.

The **view** from the cross is very rewarding – back across the amphitheatre to Velino, directly down the Valle di Teve, down the far side of the mountain to the rifugio and across the Valle Cerchiata to Piano di Pezza.

From the summit, descend north east to the **rifugio** by vague paths, steeply and uncomfortably across scree and boulders.

From the rifugio, take the path signposted Piano di Pezza ('1A'). It descends eastwards into a small valley with cliffs to the left. Soon the forest is re-entered. Descent continues to the **junction** in Valle Cerchiata passed at the start of the day. Turn left and enjoy the final stretch through the forest to the Piano.

WALK 37
Monte Ocre

Start/finish	Centre of Rocca di Cambio (42.234993, 13.489974)
Distance	16km
Total ascent/descent	1020m
Difficulty	3 (route snowbound from November to April)
Walking time	7hr
High/low points	2202m/1319m
Map	Velino-Sirente (1:25,000)
Access	The village of Rocca di Cambio lies in the northern part of the high plain, Altopiano delle Rocche, in the Sirente-Velino Regional Park. It can be approached from Celano in the south or L'Aquila in the north as it lies just off the road that connects the two. (For further details see Appendix B.)
Parking	Centre of the old village. There is a small piazza next to the church (Chiesa dell'Annunziata) on Via Duca degli Abruzzi that is good, but anywhere allowable will do.

A straightforward but most satisfying mountain circuit from the highest village in Abruzzo. The route passes gently through beech forest before crossing open moutainside to reach the summit of Monte Ocre. The view across the plain below to the city of L'Aquila with its dramatic backdrop of the high peaks of the Gran Sasso is magnificent. The fine ridge is traversed easily and includes a second peak, Monte Cagno, before a final steep descent leads back to the village.

This is a full day out in the mountains with few navigational challenges. The elevated start makes the ascent a reasonable endeavour, lending most fit walkers the opportunity to enjoy it all. Note, however, the steep descent will test the knees. Regardless, the views will stay with you for a long time!

Rocca di Cambio, situated at 1433m at the northern end of the Altopiano delle Rocche ('High Plain of the Fortresses'), is not only the highest village in Abruzzo but also the highest village in Italy outside of the Alps. The village centre is ancient; a maze of tight little streets that run into darkness between solidly built houses and churches, sometimes opening onto small courtyards and piazzas that offer unexpected vistas towards Monte Sirente way across the plain.

From the Chiesa dell'Annunziata church, continue westwards along Via Duca degli Abruzzi, past the post office on the left, to where the road leaves the old houses and descends to the left down Via Perella. Continue to a four-way road junction with an old **watering trough** on the right. Take the road ahead on the left, Via della Crocetta (brown sign to Campo Felice), which soon descends further, past the Narcisso Blu hotel, to reach the main road.

Turn right and walk along the main road westwards for 400 metres towards the wooded hillside to reach a tarmac track that goes right. There is a signpost for the bridleway to Campo Felice and for the mountain bike trail 'MTB SC-3'. Turn right and go down the track; this is the old road over the pass. Continue for 1km towards the trees.

You may wonder why the **new road** seems to disappear into the mountain – this is because there is a tunnel built to access the ski resort of Campo Felice.

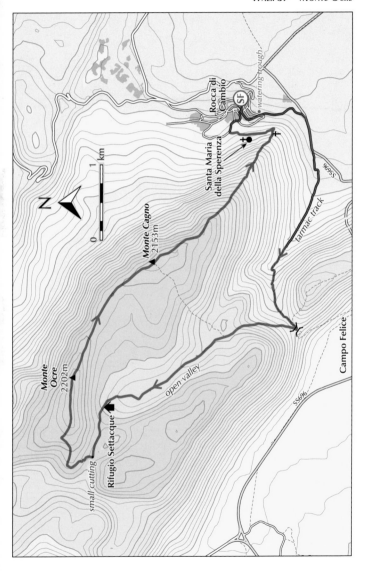

At the watering hole, with Monte Ocre behind

At the trees the tarmac ends and the old drovers' track begins. Follow it on through the patchy forest until the trees close in and the track steepens, taking a bend to the left and then crossing a clearing before emerging onto soft grassland. Climb a little further to the high point of the **pass**.

The huge **view** on the other side opens out, across the high plain of Campo Felice (its ski infrastructure mostly out of sight) towards Monte Puzzillo and Monte Cornacchia on the western skyline.

Turn right at the pass and follow a path, with occasional waymarks, that runs back across the hillside, rising slightly, and into the trees. Follow the path up through the trees and into the **open valley** that runs north east behind the Monte Ocre ridge which lies on the right.

The path continues into the treeless valley and follows it, running along the bottom, until after about 1.5km, at a small watering hole, it climbs to the rudimentary concrete hut that is **Rifugio Settacque**. ◀ The summit of Monte Ocre now lies above and to the north, but eschewing a direct line, the route continues along the 4x4 track that runs from the hut, north east, to the head of the valley.

There is a trough here that may offer the chance to refill bottles.

The track goes over a pass in a **small cutting**. Rather than continuing on the track as it descends, leave it at the pass and begin to climb the mountainside on the right. There are various small paths, but nothing asserts itself as the main way – just take a steeply rising line obliquely leftwards to reach the skyline and a rounded stony rib where the view to the north opens up.

Turn right and ascend the rib for about 150 metres, then follow a more developed path leftwards across the slope of a small corrie to a further rib on the skyline. Turn right again and walk up the broad rib, following occasional paint marks and cairns, until the ground levels and the true crest begins. Walk eastwards along the crest for 500 metres to reach the summit cross on **Monte Ocre**.

> The **view** from this 2202m vantage point is stupendous in all directions. The upper Aterno valley lies beneath the steep north east face of the mountain, with the city of L'Aquila prominent to the left. Beyond are ranged the peaks of the Corno Grande massif and the long chain above Campo Imperatore. To the south east, seemingly standing at the far end of the beautiful ridge, is Monte Sirente with its impressively craggy north east face. To the south west, Monte Velino is the obvious high point on a peak-filled horizon. All in all, a perfect lunch spot!

When suitably refreshed, begin along the lovely crest that leads south east from the summit. Walk to the summit cross of 2153m **Monte Cagno**, 1.5km away. From here continue along the crest, which soon begins a steep descent. Carefully pick your way down the obvious path, keeping on or slightly to the right of the crest. Rocca di Cambio, far below on the left, draws steadily closer; the field patterns of the wide, high plain become increasing well defined.

Just beyond another cross, the path drops into trees to the left of the ridge but then regains it to reach, finally, a third cross where it quits the crest for the last time. Take care to stay on the right path, which, as it descends, goes further south east, away from the village, but then turns back right (north) through open woodland and into trees to arrive at the chapel of **Santa Maria della Speranza**.

Continue north through trees and then fields to reach the sealed road by a small car park/yard. Turn right along the road and find your way back through the streets of **Rocca di Cambio** to your car.

Cross on the south east ridge of Monte Cagno

WALK 38
Fontecchio and Pagliare di Tione

Start/finish	Ancient village of Fontecchio in the Aterno valley (42.229889, 13.605738)
Distance	19.5km
Total ascent/descent	1000m
Difficulty	2
Walking time	6hr 30min (there are options to shorten the route)
High/low points	1116m/507m
Map	Velino-Sirente (1:25,000)
Access	Fontecchio lies halfway along the Aterno valley. It is easily reached from L'Aquila in the north or Molina Aterno in the south by the SR261 road that runs through the valley along the north east side. Molina Aterno itself can be reached from Raiano and the Sulmona valley in the south east via the Aterno gorge. It can also be reached from further west on the A25 motorway by taking the exit for Celano and then continuing, via Collarmele, to Castel di Ieri in the Subequo valley and then via Castelvecchio Subequo.
Parking	On or near Piazza del Popolo in the historic village centre

Many variations are possible on this low-level visit to Piane di Iano, one of the finest pastures in Abruzzo. The Piane feels like a remote world, surrounded by wooded slopes and cut off from civilisation. The north east wall of the Sirente dominates one side, and two semi-deserted summer villages – relics of a bygone age – bear testament to the fact that this can be a tough place. But the Aterno valley provides a strong contrast – particularly the start point of Fontecchio, which is a jewel of an old village. An alternative, avoiding a long ascent, is to drive to the Piane di Iano from Tione and make this a gentle half-day walk.

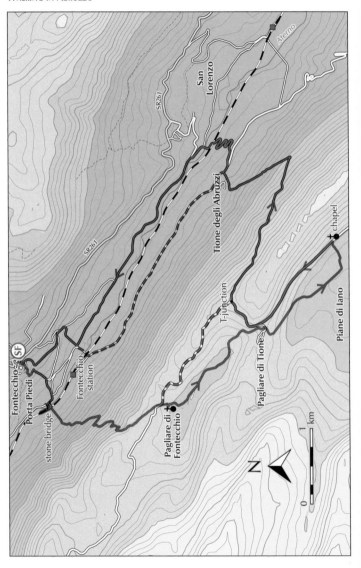

From Piazza del Popolo in **Fontecchio**, steps lead down from the beautiful old fountain to the road. Go right along the road towards old houses that overlook the valley and then, via alleys, to the furthest point out. A cobbled path leads through an ancient village gate called **Porta Piedi**. Go down overgrown steps and join the track down to the river.

Continue past a water works to reach the sealed road. Take the right fork and descend further until, to the right, you cross the river on a lovely **stone bridge**. ▶ Turn right and walk upstream for about 100 metres between the river and railway until you find a tiny, possibly rather overgrown tunnel under the line. Crouch through it to the other side. Turn left and walk downstream for 100 metres or so to a signposted path leading up into woods on the right.

An old mill stands downstream.

Follow the ancient mule track up many zig-zags as it climbs the steep and long slope. Occasional breaks in the trees allow views back to Fontecchio. Eventually the trees thin and you are on level ground. The white cross over-looking the village is a little to the right. Go ahead to the south east (leftwards) on a semi-paved way across mead-ows and through thickets to an unsealed white road. Turn

The church at Pagliare di Fontecchio

This is a peaceful place with a very old atmosphere.

left and straightaway reach a right turn to the **Pagliare di Fontecchio**. Arrive at the little restored chapel with a map board in front. ◄

> The **pagliare** of Fontecchio and Tione, now semi-derelict hamlets, were once the homes of shepherds and herders and their families in the summer months. By living here during the summer they happily avoided the trip to and from the Aterno valley each day. Both hamlets are slowly being rescued and boast recently renovated churches.

From the church, descend to the shallow Ovacchia valley, best done via houses to the left. A track leads to a little **lake**. With the lake on your right, continue south eastwards. The 4x4 track rises at the far end towards the **Pagliare di Tione**, the first houses of which appear on the skyline to the right. Arrive at the *pagilare*'s impressive central well – about 12m across and with steps descending into it. The scattered hamlet lies around. ◄

You could drive to the pagliare up the steep road from Tione degli Abruzzi and avoid most of the day's effort.

The panorama is wonderful – the Piane di Iano below, the forest beyond and the huge rocky wall of Monte Sirente that dominates the horizon.

> The high, secluded **grasslands** of Abruzzo are one of its defining features. They have provided unfenced summer grazing for sheep, horses and cattle for centuries. There are many fine examples, but the Piane di Iano is one of the best – at the height of summer it is reminiscent of a miniature African grassland rather than somewhere just 2hr from Rome.

Follow a track that leads down from the houses, through a small valley and into the centre of the plain. Wander south eastwards across the flat plain to drinking troughs and a watering hole almost below the little chapel of SS Trinita on the left. There are always grazing animals on the piano – horses, sheep and cattle. Pass without fuss and they will ignore you.

Walk to the **chapel**, passing another large well on the right before ascending the slope. There is a fine view back. From the chapel, walk north west (left) along the rising white road back to Pagliare di Tione. Stay on the road above the village, and after it bends right, follow it for a further 500 metres to a **T-junction**.

There are two ways back to Fontecchio from here. Quickest is to turn left along the white road to Pagliare di Fontecchio and from there reverse the route exactly to Fontecchio. Alternatively, for a more tiring but overall more interesting way, turn right and make the steep tarmacked descent to the village of **Tione degli Abruzzi** in the Aterno valley. The views south east down the valley are lovely. The road passes right of the historic village centre to reach a junction. ▶

Tione and Fontecchio were both badly shaken in the 2009 earthquake. Some buildings may still be shored up.

At the junction, there are two choices for the valley bottom. The quicker route is to turn left through the village and follow a quiet road that leads to Fontecchio station, staying south west of the river. Just before the station, cross the river to follow the road that climbs to the village, via big zig-zags, arriving at the steps up to Piazza del Popolo.

But if you have time and energy, the return on the north east side of the river is probably more interesting. At the junction, turn right and then left down hairpins to

Piane di Iano from the shepherds' chapel

the **River Aterno**. Cross it and go left for 100 metres until the road swings right. A lane leads ahead along the valley bottom; follow it to the junction with the road from Fontecchio station. Here you can follow the road, as above, to **Fontecchio**. Or, at a point where the road first bends right, continue ahead to the track you descended on the outward route.

WALK 39

The Navelli plain

Start/finish	Village of Prata d'Ansidonia on the Navelli plain (42.275620, 13.613028)
Distance	18.5km
Total ascent/descent	505m
Difficulty	2
Walking time	6hr
High/low points	1058m/763m
Access	Prata d'Ansidonia is south of L'Aquila and easily reached from the main SS17 road that runs from L'Aquila to Navelli (and on to Bussi and Popoli). From L'Aquila, turn off right at the village of San Pio delle Camere, about 1km beyond the Tamoil garage, and follow signs for Prata d'Ansidonia. From the south, turn off the SS17 at this same junction – it's recently been rebuilt and is especially confusing, but follow the signs and don't worry when you double back for a stretch!
Parking	Near to Bar Castello – on the left as you enter the village

An undulating, relatively gentle day's exploration of the high Navelli plain and bordering woodlands, visiting four old villages, one boasting a chapel with extraordinary frescoes. It's a route of great variety and contrast – forest and grassland, villages, chapels and quiet countryside, ruined castles and the remains of a Roman town. The way also follows an ancient sheep drove, or *tratturo*, still used today by shepherds on the flat pasture. Watch out too for crocus fields at certain times of the year – the broad Navelli plain is a centre for saffron production. This route is an excellent way to sample upland Abruzzo – it offers plenty of views but keeps comfortably below the tree line.

Note that the route is not covered by a published map. You should have no difficulties, however, using just the sketch map and description. Google Maps is a possible backup!

Left of Bar Castello, follow a lane south east towards low forested slopes in which stands the fortified hamlet of Castel Camponeschi (or Castello di Prata). Continue through the woods to the junction with the castle access road. Go left to the **castle**, looping back to climb to its gate. ▶

Restoration of the hamlet of Castel Camponeschi and its church is almost complete.

Facing away from the gate, continue south east along the white road on the left, with fine views over the Navelli plain. Pass a small lake (sometimes dried out) and continue easily to enter the village of **Tussio** below its unusual bell-tower. Cross the Piazza della Chiesa outside the church and follow the white cobbled road (Via Lauretana) that leads ahead, past houses, and then down left to meet the road up from the plain. Turn south west (right) and go up past a chapel on the left.

Just before the village cemetery (which is set back on the right), at a **metal cross**, take the track that leads left along a field edge and then swings south east (leftwards) to re-enter the forest. The way climbs steadily for a straight 1km to a small grassy saddle where the view south opens out. Cross the saddle and descend, with a field on the left, towards **Bominaco**.

Turn left at the first junction onto a track that climbs to the castle tower on the skyline. Enter the ruins of **Bominaco Castle**, the high point of the walk, and admire the wonderful views, particularly north east towards the main peaks of the Gran Sasso. ▶ Leave the castle and turn left down a stepped path to the chapel below.

This is a fine spot for a picnic.

This is the **San Pellegrino Oratory** – lovely outside but splendid on the inside, with frescoes covering nearly all of the walls. Unfortunately it is kept locked, but there may be a guide present. There is a phone number outside to ask someone to let you in. A café in the corner of the open space on the right is sometimes open.

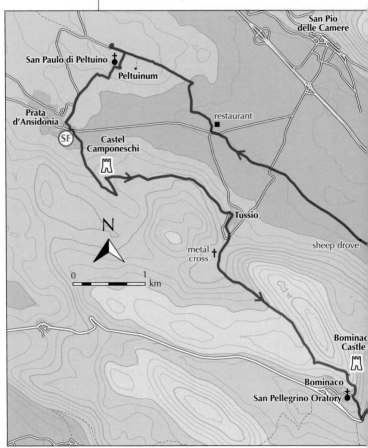

The route now heads down to Caporciano about 1km away to the north east. Follow the sign from the oratory and descend rightwards, along a marked path, to the road. Walk down the quiet road, passing a cemetery on the left, to arrive at **Caporciano**. The road turns right and enters the village. Follow Via Roma to the main piazza.

From the piazza, turn sharply north west (left) and walk out of the village on a tarmac road that descends, via one right-hand hairpin, to arrive at a crossroads on the plain. Turn left to start along a sealed lane north westwards. The lane runs initially between trees but soon the

Caporciano and the Navelli plain

231

About 600 metres before the road, a lane leads left to Tussio and another then runs along the base of the woods back to the start – a way to shorten the day if you're not interested in Roman ruins.

fields open out. You are now on the old **sheep drove** (*tratturo*). Follow it across the level plain until you reach a tarmacked road that descends from Tussio. ◀

Cross the road and continue along the lane. In 200 metres cross another road and continue in the same direction. The lane bears slightly right and finishes at the road to Prata d'Ansidonia. Turn left along the road for about 100 metres and then right to a **restaurant** (Settefonti). Follow the track around the left of the building and go left behind a caravan site (possibly disused). Keeping trees to the left, reach a larger white lane. Turn right and follow it, climbing slowly, to another path junction.

The plateau on which **Peltuinum** stands is to the north west (left). Turn left and follow the broad sheep drove up to the promontory. Beyond a parking area on the left lie extensive excavations. Some are accessible, but the further ones may not be (the dig is still active).

When you've explored, return to the main drove and walk to the few standing walls of the old north west gate. Retrace your steps for 200 metres to turn down a track on the right (when walking back from the gate), which runs between and then across fields. It then leads south east before swinging right, down to the **San Paulo di Peltuino chapel** under the bank. From the door, follow the track further down as it turns first left and then right between fields.

Where it joins another track that arrives from the left, go right. A little further on, at a junction with another track, turn left and follow it for 300 metres to the road. Turn left along the road to reach **Prata d'Ansidonia**.

THE SIMBRUINI
REGIONAL PARK

The ridge leading to Monte Viglio with the
gendarme straddling the way (Walk 40)

WALK 40

Monte Viglio

Start/finish	Passo Serra Sant'Antonio, south west of Capistrello (41.918420, 13.368759)
Distance	12.5km
Total ascent/descent	935m
Difficulty	3 (route snowbound from November to April)
Walking time	5hr 30min
High/low points	2156m/1574m
Map	Simbruini (1:25,000)
Access	Ease of access will depend on the condition of the road on the Abruzzo (east) side of the pass. From Capistrello, take the SP30 that climbs for a steep and winding 20km to the pass. This is the Via Salustio as you leave the town, becoming the Via Simbruina. (In 2017 the road was indicated to be closed due to its poor condition, but in fact it was drivable in a regular car all the way to the pass, albeit with a few potholes.) Should the road be unusable, the only other way is up from the Lazio side, on a much better road. This is the SP28 which goes into the Valle Granara from Altipiani di Arcinazzo, via Filettino. Above Filettino the road to the pass is the SP30.
Parking	On the pass

A wonderful walk in the secluded and scarce-visited Simbruini mountains, taking in the crest that forms the border of Abruzzo and Lazio, with Monte Viglio proudly serving as the high point. This is the furthest west of all the routes in this guide – in fact you will find yourself inside Lazio for more than half the journey – and it stands alone.

The route comprises a satisfying balance of ancient woodland, pasture, cliffs, a rocky ridge, a fine peak and silent forest. Starting at almost 1600m, the way rises steadily on good tracks and paths to reach its 2156m peak with relative ease. (The ridge offers a direct and entertaining ascent over a large gendarme, but if you don't want to use your hands it is easily bypassed.)

The ridge walk continues beyond the summit, with outstanding views, and then after an initially steep descent the return leg is a very pleasant, gently undulating stroll through forest – a relaxing end to a grand day!

From the pass, set off along a wide 4x4 track that heads south east into woodland. There is a signpost at the beginning – as indicated, follow path 651 towards Monte Viglio. The unsealed road, used by loggers and herders, runs to the right of the ridge, with slight rises and falls, leading to **Fonte della Moscosa** about 1.2km away. The track forks at a signpost near the drinking trough; go left and follow path 696a (Monte Viglio) as it climbs up and into a beautiful elongated meadow that lies between wooded slopes.

Walk along the track to the far end of the meadow and then climb again, back into trees. The path leads quickly to a magnificent viewpoint on the ridge with a **cross**, a Madonna and a stone table. The views down to the Liri valley and across into the mountains of the Abruzzo National Park are wonderful.

Go right (looking east) from the cross and continue on the good path, southwards, through thin woodland

Out onto the hillside with the summit of I Cantari to the left

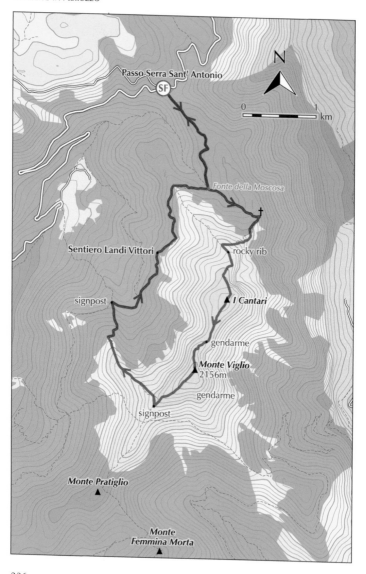

just back from the ridge itself. The path drops slightly before swinging right onto the open hillside, which it ascends obliquely across the slope towards a rocky rib on the right skyline. Take the higher of the two paths to the rib.

When you reach the **rocky rib**, turn left and ascend easily towards the small saddle ahead, admiring the very fine views developing in every direction – particularly of the grand cliffs that drop from the first peak on the ridge, I Cantari. Halfway along, pass the junction with path 651, which joins from the right.

At the saddle the way swings rightwards and then left to stay on the main crest. The most developed path passes to the right of **I Cantari** with its statue of a saint (which you might have thought was a real person earlier – worth a quick diversion to assure yourself it is inanimate). The path runs easily on towards the now obvious summit of Monte Viglio.

A **gendarme** straddling the ridge appears ahead, blocking the way to the summit. If you would rather not scramble over it, take the well-trod path that runs parallel to the ridge but 10 metres to its right – visible on approach. This bears away to pass to the right of the gendarme and rejoins the ridge on the far side.

If you are happy to go over the gendarme (it's not hard but you need to pull up a few times), stay on the ridge, and just right of the crest follow the path steeply up and over the rocks.

Once beyond the gendarme, ascend the fine crest to the summit cross of **Monte Viglio**, where another statue of the Madonna, a little below, makes a fine lunch spot.

Now continue south west down the summit slope and along the broad ridge to a signpost at a protuberance about 600 metres away. At the **signpost** go sharp right, almost an about-turn, to follow the level path 696b (Sentiero Landi Vittori) as it contours back across the west slope of the mountain to reach a rib about 150 metres away. At the rib, turn left and follow it down on the occasionally vague path, without deviating, all the way to the trees. ▶

The view to the right in particular, into the wild corrie on the west face of Monte Viglio, is very fine.

The west face of Monte Viglio from the descent rib

Enter the forest, taking great care to remain on the path, which becomes indistinct. While the path still decends, it now goes obliquely to the right of the ridge line. Drop steeply to reach a **signpost** at the junction with path 654, the much better-defined Sentiero Landi Vittori, which contours the mountainside in the forest. (If you lose the descent path, don't worry – make your own way steeply down, trending rightwards, and you will soon find yourself on path 654, which lies 150m lower than the treeline. Look out for it.)

Once on the **Sentiero Landi Vittori**, turn right and follow it with much delight, overall north eastwards, back towards Fonte della Moscosa, about 2km away. The old mule track takes a fine line, turning in and out of a number of small stream valleys dropping from the ridge, rising and falling a little, and passing at times across pasture just above the trees.

A little before **Fonte della Moscosa**, the Sentiero merges with path 651 and the combined way soon arrives back at the picnic tables and trough. From here reverse your earlier steps back along the unsealed road to **Passo Serra Sant'Antonio**.

APPENDIX A
Route summary table

Walk	Start point	Area	Distance	Asent/descent	Difficulty	Time	Page
1 Fara San Martino gorge and Val Serviera	Fara San Martino	Maiella National Park	16.5km	2100m	3	7hr 30min	37
2 The hermitage of San Bartolomeo di Legio	Decontra	Maiella National Park	5.5km	280m	1	2hr 30min	42
3 Monte Morrone from Passo San Leonardo	Passo San Leonardo	Maiella National Park	19.5km	1370m	2	6hr 30min	46
4 Morrone di Pacentro and Monte Mileto	Pacentro village	Maiella National Park	19.5km	1555m	2	7hr	51
5 The Orfento valley	Caramanico Terme	Maiella National Park	17.5km	1390m	2	6hr	56
6 Caramanico and the Orfento gorge	Caramanico Terme	Maiella National Park	4km	215m	1	2hr	60
7 Monte Amaro from Lama Bianca	Lama Biancha road head, near Sant'Eufemia a Maiella	Maiella National Park	8.5km	1315m	3	6hr 30min	64
8 Monte Amaro from La Maielletta	La Maielletta	Maiella National Park	24.5km	1700m	3	8hr 30min	68
9 Monte Amaro from Fonte Romana	Near Fonte Romana	Maiella National Park	22.5km	1655m	3	8hr	73

Walk	Start point	Area	Distance	Asent/descent	Difficulty	Time	Page
10 The Alento valley above Serramonacesca	Serramonacesca	Maiella National Park	9.5km	430m	1	3hr 30min	78
11 Monte Porrara ridge	Palena railway station	Maiella National Park	14.5km	1045m/1235m	3	6hr 30min	83
12 Monte Prena and Monte Camicia	Fonte Vetica	Corno Grande and Campo Imperatore	14.5km	1410m	3	8hr	91
13 Santo Stefano and Rocca Calascio	Santo Stefano di Sessanio	Corno Grande and Campo Imperatore	10km	440m	1	4hr	96
14 The west summit of Corno Grande	Campo Imperatore hotel	Corno Grande and Campo Imperatore	10.5km	1080m	3	6hr 30min	101
15 The east summit of Corno Grande	Prati di Tivo	Corno Grande and Campo Imperatore	7km	1060m	3	6hr 30min	106
16 Campo Pericoli and Pizzo Cefalone	Campo Imperatore hotel	Corno Grande and Campo Imperatore	13km	1205m	3	6hr 30min	111
17 Monte Bolza ridge	Campo Imperatore	Corno Grande and Campo Imperatore	14.5km	640m	2	6hr	116
18 Pietracamela and Prati di Tivo	Pietracamela	Corno Grande and Campo Imperatore	7.5km	455m	1	4hr	121
19 Monte Corvo and the Val Chiarino	Lago di Provvidenza	Corno Grande and Campo Imperatore	23.5km	1810m	3	8hr	125
20 Monte di Mezzo circuit from Campotosto	Campotosto	Monti Della Laga	16.5km	995m	3	7hr	132

Walk	Start point	Area	Distance	Asent/descent	Difficulty	Time	Page
21 Cima della Laghetta and Monte Gorzano	Cesacastina	Monti Della Laga	18km	1510m	3	7hr 30min	137
22 Villetta Barrea and Civitella Alfedena	Villetta Barrea	Abruzzo National Park	8km	345m	1	4hr	145
23 The Val di Rose	Civitella Alfedena	Abruzzo National Park	12.5km	985m	3	6hr	148
24 Monte La Meta and the Mainarde crest	Pianora Campitelli	Abruzzo National Park	17.5km	1160m	3	7hr	153
25 La Terratta	Scanno	Abruzzo National Park	14km	1295m	3	6hr 30min	158
26 The Scanno town and lake loop	Scanno	Abruzzo National Park	8km	375m	1	3hr	162
27 Serra del Campitello and Monte Godi	Near Passo Godi	Abruzzo National Park	25km	1290m	3	7hr	166
28 Monte Marsicano	Pescasseroli	Abruzzo National Park	20km	1265m	3	7hr	172
29 Colli Alti and Bassi from Pescasseroli	Pescasseroli	Abruzzo National Park	18.5km	660m	2	6hr	177
30 Anversa degli Abruzzi and Castrovalva	Anversa degli Abruzzi	Sulmona Valley and Monte Genzana	7km	555m	1	3hr	184
31 Monte Mattone from Pettorano sul Gizio	Pettorano	Sulmona Valley and Monte Genzana	12.5km	1030m	2	4hr 30min	189

Walk	Start point	Area	Distance	Asent/descent	Difficulty	Time	Page
32 Monte Genzana from Pettorano sul Gizio	Pettorano	Sulmona Valley and Monte Genzana	20km	1750m	3	7hr 30min	191
33 A tour of the Valle del Gizio	Near Sulmona	Sulmona Valley and Monte Genzana	17.5km	805m	2	6hr	197
34 Monte Sirente	Chalet Sirente rifugio between Secinaro and Rocca di Mezzo	Sirente-Velino Regional Park	9.5km	1155m	3	6hr	205
35 The Celano gorge via Fonte degli Innamorati	Near Celano	Sirente-Velino Regional Park	10.5km	1155m	2	5hr 30min	209
36 Monte Velino	Capo Pezza	Sirente-Velino Regional Park	20km	1515m	3	7hr 30min	212
37 Monte Ocre	Rocca di Cambio	Sirente-Velino Regional Park	16km	1020m	3	7hr	217
38 Fontecchio and Pagliare di Tione	Fontecchio	Sirente-Velino Regional Park	19.5km	1000m	2	6hr 30min	223
39 The Navelli plain	Prata d'Ansidonia	Sirente-Velino Regional Park	18.5km	505m	2	6hr	228
40 Monte Viglio	Passo Serra Sant'Antonio	The Simbruini Regional Park	12.5km	935m	3	5hr 30min	234

APPENDIX B

Further access information

Walk 2

From the south, the road winds down from the San Leonardo pass to Caramanico via the village of Sant'Eufemia. Bypass the town centre through two tunnels. About 600 metres after the second tunnel, turn right up a side road signposted for Riga and Decontra. Decontra lies 6km along this road. Passo San Leonardo itself is reached going east from Sulmona via Campo di Giove.

From the north, turn off the SS5 at Scafa and take the SR487 signposted for San Valentino and Caramanico. Some 500 metres before the first roundabout for Caramanico, turn left up the side road signposted for Riga and Decontra.

Walk 3

From Campo di Giove, head north towards the pass and Caramanico until you reach the junction with the SR487 (closed at the time of writing) after about 8km. Continue ahead and in a further 2km reach the lodge and restaurant on the pass.

From Caraminico, take the SR487 south up the wide valley, passing through Sant'Eufemia, before ascending a further 8km to the pass. (Caramanico itself is reached from the Pescara valley via the village of San Valentino. Turn off the SS5 main road at Scafa and follow the SR487.)

Note that there is a road from Pacentro to Passo San Leonardo, the SR487, which climbs from the village via a set of steep hairpins to reach the central valley in about 8km, where the way from Campo di Giove joins from the right. The road is currently closed awaiting the completion of stabilisation work but hopefully will soon be reopened.

Walks 5 and 6

From the south, the road winds down from the San Leonardo pass to Caramanico via the village of Sant'Eufemia. At the first roundabout on reaching the town, take the road for the town centre. (If you enter a tunnel you've overshot, but there's a roundabout at the far end and another turn for the centre.) Passo San Leonardo itself is reached going east from Sulmona via Campo di Giove.

From the north, turn off the SS5 at Scafa and follow the SR487 signposted to San Valentino and Caramancio. At Caramanico, after crossing the bridge over the gorge, reach a roundabout just before the road tunnel. Turn left for the town centre.

Walk 8

From Roccamorice, take the road south west up the hill signposted for Santo Spirito and Blockhaus. After about 4km, the road forks. The road right continues into the Santo Spirito valley. Fork left, for Blockhaus, and steadily climb a narrow mountain road to the ski lifts about 8km away. (Roccamorice is best reached from the SS5 at Scafa via the town of San Valentino.)

From Lettomanoppello, take the road south and then south west signposted for Passo Lanciano. Reach the Passo in about 9km. From here go up a further 3km to the Maielletta. (Lettomanoppello is also best reached from the SS5 near Scafa, the junction being nearer Pescara and Chieti.)

From Pretoro, take the winding road south westwards for about 5km up to Passo Lanciano. From the Passo continue up to Maielletta. (Pretoro is the best approach if arriving from the east and north east – Pescara, Chieti and points along the coast.)

From the first lodges on the slopes, drive up the hairpins of the resurfaced road to the upper rifugios and telecommunication masts.

Walk 11

For **Campo di Giove**, leave Sulmona by the SR487 towards Pacentro. After 6km the road to Campo di Giove, via Cansano, turns off right. Turn right as you enter the village for the station.

Palena station is reached by road from Campo di Giove by going eastwards out of the village towards the small ski resort of Le Piane. Continue beyond the ski resort and over a low pass to the Quarto Santa Chiara.

Walk 12, 14, 16 and 17

Castel del Monte is reached from the Sulmona and Popoli area by following the SS17 road north towards L'Aquila and turning right to the village of Ofena just beyond left turns to Capestrano. The road goes through Ofena and then, after turning left, through Santa Lucia degli Abruzzi before climbing to Castel del Monte. Pass through the village and take the road on the north side for Campo

Imperatore. About 3km after dropping to the vast plain a junction is reached with a wooden building either side of the road. Turn right down the straight road for 2km to Fonte Vetica.

From the village of **Assergi**, north east of L'Aquila, follow the road to the motorway. Go beyond the motorway for almost 1km and turn right for Fonte Cerreto. The road passes the cable car station to wind up to Campo Imperatore. About 12km from Fonte Cerreto a turn left goes to the Campo Imperatore hotel, but continue ahead towards Castel del Monte. Reach the junction and wooden buildings in about 8km. Turn left to Fonte Vetica.

If you take the road up from **Santo Stefano**, turn right at the T-junction on the campo to reach the wooden buildings in about 5km. If coming up from **Farindola**, via Rigopiano, turn right on the Campo, at the T-junction with the road coming up from Castel del Monte, to reach the wooden buildings.

Walk 13

Turn off the **SS17** for Barisciano. Pass through Barisciano, following the road for Calascio and Castel del Monte that climbs above. It passes Santo Stefano in about 8km.

Two other ways lead to Santo Stefano – approach from **Calascio** in the opposite direction (which itself can be reached separately from the south) or descend the long (and beautiful) road from the heart of **Campo Imperatore**.

Walk 20

Coming **from Teramo**, turn off right (northwards) at the village of Ortolano and follow a twisting road for a few kilometres to reach the reservoir. Turn right and follow the lakeside road to reach Campotosto in 6km.

Coming **from L'Aquila**, turn off left on a road signposted for the reservoir and village about 4km after reaching the plateau of Passo delle Campannelle. The road runs to the retaining wall of the reservoir and then rightwards alongside its twisting margin to the village about 10km further on.

Walk 22

From **Castel di Sangro**, take the SS17, the main north–south route through Abruzzo, then the SS83 about 3km south of Castel di Sangro, signposted to Pescasseroli. Pass through Alfedena and continue through Barrea before dropping to the lakeside, along which the road continues for 3.5km to reach Villetta at the far end.

Villetta can also be reached from the opposite direction by taking the SS83 from **Pescasseroli**. Additionally, Villetta can be reached from **Scanno**, 15km to the north, by taking the twisting SR479 over the Passo Godi. At the junction with the SS83, turn right to Villetta.

Walk 23

Access is via the SS83, the main road that passes through the park along the Upper Sangro valley. Depending on the direction you approach from, take one of two routes to Civitella.

From the SS17, the main north–south route through Abruzzo, take the SS83 about 3km south of Castel di Sangro, signposted for Pescasseroli. Pass through Alfedena and continue through Barrea before dropping to the lakeside, along which the road continues for 3.5km to reach, at the far end, the turn for Civitella on the left. Cross the bridge

over the lake and climb a hairpinned road to the village.

Approaching **from the north west**, along the SS83 from Pescasseroli, enter the village of Villetta Barrea and, in about 400 metres, take the turn on the right signposted for Civitella. This crosses the Sangro river and climbs through forest to enter the lower part of the village.

It is also possible to reach Villetta **from Scanno**, 15km to the north, by taking the twisting SR479 over the Passo Godi. At the junction with the SS83, either turn left and after 1km turn right to Civitella; or turn right and pass through Villetta to turn left to Civitella after 500 metres.

Walk 24

Alfedena is halfway along the SS83 between Barrea to the west and its junction with the SS17 to the east. This junction is 3km south of Castel di Sangro.

From the centre of Alfedena, drive towards Barrea and in 300 metres take a turn on the left (Via del Lago) at the first big bend to the right. Look for a sign to 'Azienda Agrituristica Rio Torto'. Drive up Via del Largo for 3.5km to a junction with a road on the right. There is a sign for Pianora Campitelli. Turn right up this road, which twists and turns up through the forest for 6km to emerge at the large pasture of Pianora Campitelli with the rifugio at its far end.

Walk 27

Reach Scanno **from the north** after passing through the narrow Sagittario gorge on the SR479 from Anversa degli Abruzzi and the Sulmona valley. Passo Godi is 15km south of Scanno on the same road.

From the south, on the SS17, take the SS83 about 3km south of Castel di Sangro, signposted for Pescasseroli. Pass through Alfedena and continue through Barrea before dropping to the lakeside, along which the road continues for 4km to reach Villetta Barrea. From there turn right and take the SR479 north for about 14km to Passo Godi.

Walks 28 and 29

From the north west the SS83 runs from Pescina, just south of the A25 motorway. Take the exit for Pescina. The road runs south east along the side of the flat Fucinio basin, passing through Gioia dei Marsi, before rising to enter the Abruzzo National Park, passing the village of Gioia Vecchio. Pescasseroli can also be reached from Ortona dei Marsi in the north west.

From the south east the SS83 runs through the heart of the park from near Castel di Sangro, passing through Alfedena, Barrea, Villetta Barrea and Opi.

Walk 36

From the north (L'Aquila), pass through the centre of Rocca di Mezzo until a turn on the right, at a roundabout near the Albergo Caldora, leads for about 4km to the Piano (Via di Pezza). The tarmac road ends at a large car park overlooking the long meadow. Follow the unsealed road, which goes to the left and then around the back of the new rifugio to descend onto the plain. Drive carefully; the way is potholed. Follow the road slowly for 5km across the golden grass.

From the south, join the road between Rocca di Mezzo and the Piano via a lane from Rovere. Roughly in the centre of the lower part of Rovere, turn left from the main road to Rocca di Mezzo to follow a lane (possibly signposted 'pic nic') for about 2km to the junction.

Walk 37

From Celano, take the SS696, via Ovindoli, to reach Rocca di Cambio, 27km to the north. **From L'Aquila**, take the SS5bis, via San Felice d'Ocre, to reach Rocca di Cambio, 26km to the south. Drive into the centre of the old village. The village can also be reached from the Campo Felice ski area to the west.

APPENDIX C

Italian–English glossary

abbazia	abbey
acqua (non) potabile	(un)drinkable water
affittacamere	B&B
agriturismo	farm stay
aiuto!	help!
albergo	hotel
albero	tree
alto	high
anello	ring
autobus	bus
autostazione	bus station
basso	low
bivio	fork, junction
borgo	village, small town
bosco	wood
cabine	cable car
caduta sassi	rockfalls
camere libere	rooms available
campo	field
canale	gully
capanna, casale, casotto	hut
casa	house
cascata	waterfall
castello	castle
catena	chain
chiesa	church
cima	mountain peak
cimitero	cemetery
colle	hill
cresta, crinale	ridge
croce	cross
davanti a	in front of
destra	right
dietro	behind
dificile	difficult
di fronte a	facing
diga	dam
erboso	grassy
eremo	hermitage
escursione	hike
est/orientale	east/eastern
faggio	beech wood
facile	easy
fermata	bus stop
ferrovia	railway
fiore	flower
fiume	river
fonte, fontanile	spring (water)
forca	col, pass
foresta	forest
forra	ravine
fosso	lit. ditch, but used for valley and watercourse
frana	landslide, landslip
frazione	hamlet
funivia	cable car
gelo	frost, freeze
ghiacciaio	glacier
ghiaccio	ice
giro	turn, tour
gola	gorge, canyon
grotta	cave
incrocio	crossroads, intersection

in ritardo	late	*punta*	point, mountain peak
lago	lake		
lontano	far	*quercia*	oak
maneggio	horse-riding	*rifugio*	mountain hut or inn
monte	mountain		
mulattiera	mule track	*ripido*	steep
municipio	local council	*rocca*	fortress
nebbia	fog	*roccioso*	rocky
neve	snow	*sede*	headquarters
nord/settentrionale	north/northern	*segui*	follow
orario	timetable	*sella*	saddle, col
ospedale	hospital	*sentiero*	walking path
ovest/occidentale	west/western	*sempre diritto*	straight ahead
paese	village	*sereno*	sunny
pantano	bog	*sinistra*	left
parcheggio	car park	*soccorso alpino*	mountain rescue
passeggiata	promenade, walk		
		sole	sun
passarella pedonale	footbridge	*sorgente*	spring (water)
pedonale	for pedestrians	*stazione ferrovia*	railway station
pendici	mountain slopes	*sterrata*	dirt road
percorso	route	*strada*	road
pericolo/pericoloso	danger/dangerous	*stretta*	narrow valley
		sud/meridionale	south/southern
piano	plain, plateau (noun) or slowly, quietly	*tempo*	weather
		temporale	thunderstorm
		tornante	hairpin bend
piazza	town square	*torre*	tower
pioggia	rain	*torrente*	mountain stream
pizzo	mountain peak, point		
		val, valle, vallon, vallone	valley
poggio	modest mountain, hilltop	*valanga*	avalanche
ponte	bridge	*vento*	wind
pozzo	well	*vetta*	peak
prato	meadow, field	*via*	way, road
presto	early	*vicino*	near
Pro Loco	local tourist office		
pullman	bus		

APPENDIX D
Useful contacts

Travel

Pescara airport
www.abruzzoairport.com

Rome airports www.adr.it

Ancona airport
www.aeroportomarche.it

Napoli airport
www.aeroportodinapoli.it

Italian railways (TrenItala)
www.trenitalia.com

Abruzzo buses (Italian only)
www.tuabruzzo.it
www.prontobusitalia.it

Alitalia www.alitalia.com

Blue Air www.blueairweb.com

British Airways
www.britishairways.com

Easyjet www.easyjet.com

Flybe www.flybe.com

Lufthansa www.lufthansa.com

Jet2.com www.jet2.com

Mistral Air www.mistralair.it

Ryanair www.ryanair.com

Wizz Air https://wizzair.com

Accommodation and information on Abruzzo

Italian tourist board
www.italiantourism.com

Abruzzo tourist board
www.abruzzoturismo.it

Hotels www.tripadvisor.co.uk

Holiday apartments
www.holidaylettings.co.uk

Campsites www.camping.it

Agriturismo www.agriturismo.it

Beautiful villages www.borghitalia.it

Things Abruzzo
www.lifeinabruzzo.com,
www.lifeinitaly.com

General guidebook *Abruzzo* by Luciano Di Gregorio (published by Bradt)

Eating

Abruzzo food
www.rusticocooking.com

Abruzzo restaurants
www.tripadvisor.co.uk

Slow food (born in Italy!)
www.slowfood.com

Walking in Abruzzo

The Abruzzo National Park
www.parcoabruzzo.it

The Gran Sasso National Park
www.gransassolagapark.it

The Maiella National Park
www.parcomajella.it

The Sirente-Velino Regional Park
www.parcosirentevelino.it

Monte Genzana Reserve
www.riservagenzana.it

Other Abruzzo nature reserves
www.parks.it/regione.abruzzo/

Club Alpino Italiano   www.cai.it

Edizioni Il Lupo   www.edizioniillupo.it

Appennini 2000 (Italian only)
www.club2000m.it

Forestry/environmental department
www.corpoforestale.it

Emergencies

Police tel 113

Mountain rescue tel 118

British embassy
http://ukinitaly.fco.gov.uk,
tel (39) 06 4220 0001

US embassy
http://it.usembassy.gov,
tel (39) 06 4674 1

Canadian embassy
www.canadainternational.gc.ca/
italy-italie,
tel (39) 06 85444 2911

Australian embassy
www.italy.embassy.gov.au,
tel (39) 06 8527 21

New Zealand embassy
www.mfat.govt.nz,
tel (39) 06 8537 501

South African embassy
www.sudafrica.it,
tel (39) 06 8525 41

DOWNLOAD THE ROUTES
IN GPX FORMAT

All the routes in this guide are available for download from:

www.cicerone.co.uk/978/GPX

as GPX files. You should be able to load them into most formats of mobile device, whether GPS or smartphone.

When you go to this link, you will be asked for your email address and where you purchased the guide, and have the option to subscribe to the Cicerone e-newsletter.

CICERONE
www.cicerone.co.uk

The Great Outdoors

DIGITAL EDITIONS
30-DAY
FREE TRIAL

- Substantial savings on the newsstand price and print subscriptions
- Instant access wherever you are, even if you are offline
- Back issues at your fingertips

Downloading **The Great Outdoors** to your digital device is easy, just follow the steps below:

1 **Download the App** from the App Store

2 **Open the App**, click on 'subscriptions' and choose an annual subscription

3 **Download** the latest issue and enjoy

The digital edition is also available on

The 30-day free trial is not available on Android or Pocketmags and is only available to new subscribers

LISTING OF CICERONE GUIDES

SCOTLAND

Backpacker's Britain:
Northern Scotland
Ben Nevis and Glen Coe
Cycling in the Hebrides
Great Mountain Days in Scotland
Mountain Biking in Southern and
Central Scotland
Mountain Biking in West and North
West Scotland
Not the West Highland Way
Scotland
Scotland's Best Small Mountains
Scotland's Mountain Ridges
Scrambles in Lochaber
The Ayrshire and Arran
Coastal Paths
The Border Country
The Cape Wrath Trail
The Great Glen Way
The Great Glen Way Map Booklet
The Hebridean Way
The Hebrides
The Isle of Mull
The Isle of Skye
The Skye Trail
The Southern Upland Way
The Speyside Way
The Speyside Way Map Booklet
The West Highland Way
Walking Highland Perthshire
Walking in Scotland's Far North
Walking in the Angus Glens
Walking in the Cairngorms
Walking in the Ochils, Campsie
Fells and Lomond Hills
Walking in the Pentland Hills
Walking in the Southern Uplands
Walking in Torridon
Walking Loch Lomond and
the Trossachs
Walking on Arran
Walking on Harris and Lewis
Walking on Rum and the
Small Isles
Walking on the Orkney and
Shetland Isles
Walking on Uist and Barra
Walking the Corbetts
Vol 1 South of the Great Glen
Walking the Corbetts
Vol 2 North of the Great Glen
Walking the Galloway Hills
Walking the Munros
Vol 1 – Southern, Central and
Western Highlands

Walking the Munros
Vol 2 – Northern Highlands and
the Cairngorms
West Highland Way Map Booklet
Winter Climbs Ben Nevis and
Glen Coe
Winter Climbs in the Cairngorms

NORTHERN ENGLAND TRAILS

Hadrian's Wall Path
Hadrian's Wall Path Map Booklet
Pennine Way Map Booklet
The Coast to Coast Map Booklet
The Coast to Coast Walk
The Dales Way
The Dales Way Map Booklet
The Pennine Way

LAKE DISTRICT

Cycling in the Lake District
Great Mountain Days in the
Lake District
Lake District Winter Climbs
Lake District: High Level and
Fell Walks
Lake District: Low Level and
Lake Walks
Mountain Biking in the Lake District
Scrambles in the Lake District
– North
Scrambles in the Lake District
– South
Short Walks in Lakeland Books 1–3
The Cumbria Way
Tour of the Lake District
Trail and Fell Running in the
Lake District

NORTH WEST ENGLAND
AND THE ISLE OF MAN

Cycling the Pennine Bridleway
Cycling the Way of the Roses
Isle of Man Coastal Path
The Lancashire Cycleway
The Lune Valley and Howgills
The Ribble Way
Walking in Cumbria's Eden Valley
Walking in Lancashire
Walking in the Forest of Bowland
and Pendle
Walking on the Isle of Man
Walking on the West
Pennine Moors
Walks in Lancashire Witch Country
Walks in Ribble Country
Walks in Silverdale and Arnside

NORTH EAST ENGLAND,
YORKSHIRE DALES AND
PENNINES

Cycling in the Yorkshire Dales
Great Mountain Days in
the Pennines
Mountain Biking in the
Yorkshire Dales
South Pennine Walks
St Oswald's Way and
St Cuthbert's Way
The Cleveland Way and the
Yorkshire Wolds Way
The Cleveland Way Map Booklet
The North York Moors
The Reivers Way
The Teesdale Way
Walking in County Durham
Walking in Northumberland
Walking in the North Pennines
Walking in the Yorkshire Dales:
North and East
Walking in the Yorkshire Dales:
South and West
Walks in Dales Country
Walks in the Yorkshire Dales

WALES AND WELSH BORDERS

Cycling Lôn Las Cymru
Glyndwr's Way
Great Mountain Days in Snowdonia
Hillwalking in Shropshire
Hillwalking in Wales – Vols 1 & 2
Mountain Walking in Snowdonia
Offa's Dyke Map Booklet
Offa's Dyke Path
Pembrokeshire Coast Path
Map Booklet
Ridges of Snowdonia
Scrambles in Snowdonia
The Ascent of Snowdon
The Ceredigion and Snowdonia
Coast Paths
The Pembrokeshire Coast Path
The Severn Way
The Snowdonia Way
The Wales Coast Path
The Wye Valley Walk
Walking in Carmarthenshire
Walking in Pembrokeshire
Walking in the Forest of Dean
Walking in the South Wales Valleys
Walking in the Wye Valley
Walking on the Brecon Beacons
Walking on the Gower
Welsh Winter Climbs

For full information on all our
guides, books and eBooks,
visit our website:
www.cicerone.co.uk

Walking – Trekking – Mountaineering – Climbing – Cycling

Over 40 years, Cicerone have built up an outstanding collection of over 300 guides, inspiring all sorts of amazing adventures.

 Every guide comes from extensive exploration and research by our expert authors, all with a passion for their subjects. They are frequently praised, endorsed and used by clubs, instructors and outdoor organisations.

All our titles can now be bought as **e-books**, **ePubs** and **Kindle** files and we also have an online magazine – **Cicerone Extra** – with features to help cyclists, climbers, walkers and trekkers choose their next adventure, at home or abroad.

Our website shows any **new information** we've had in since a book was published. Please do let us know if you find anything has changed, so that we can publish the latest details. On our **website** you'll also find great ideas and lots of detailed information about what's inside every guide and you can buy **individual routes** from many of them online.

It's easy to keep in touch with what's going on at Cicerone by getting our monthly **free e-newsletter**, which is full of offers, competitions, up-to-date information and topical articles. You can subscribe on our home page and also follow us on **Facebook** and **Twitter** or dip into our **blog**.

Cicerone – the very best guides for exploring the world.

CICERONE

Juniper House, Murley Moss, Oxenholme Road, Kendal, Cumbria LA9 7RL
Tel: 015395 62069 info@cicerone.co.uk
www.cicerone.co.uk